THE ATTACK ON KIT-HAN-NE

KITTANNING, PENNSYLVANIA
SEPTEMBER 8, 1756

BY
LARRY A. SMAIL

Front Cover
"Blanket Hill Night, September 7, 1756" by Larry A. Smail
To see other paintings by Larry Smail, visit:
www.larrysmailart.com

Published by

MECHLING BOOKBINDERY

1124 Oneida Valley Road – Route 38
Chicora, PA 16025-3820
www.mechlingbooks.com
1-800-941-3735

Copyright©2006
Larry A. Smail

Illustrations by Larry A. Smail
Edited by Marla K. Mechling
Layout and Design by Kari McConnell

No part of this publication may be copied or electronically reproduced by any means, without prior written permission from the publisher.

Printed July 2006 in the United States of America

ISBN-13: 978-0-9760563-8-6
ISBN-10: 0-9760563-8-0

Library of Congress Control Number: 2006929478

DEDICATION

The author wishes to dedicate this book to a select group of loved ones:

To my father, Allen K. Smail (1923-1999), who instilled in me a love of the natural world and an interest in history. He always found time to take me to the woods or stream.

To my mother, Ruth E. Smail, who always placed family first. She made certain that I was introduced to the Holy Word as a boy, for which I am grateful.

To my sister, Ruthie Smail, who turned out rather normal despite my attempts to do otherwise. She supplied most of the photos for this endeavor.

To my wife, Lauranne (Laurie), for understanding my needs to go the woods, occasionally "play" long hunter and vent my creative urges. I love her.

Author Larry Smail preparing to shoot his musket. He is dressed in long hunter garb. (Dad would have loved this!)
Photo by Randy Quinn

TABLE OF CONTENTS

INTRODUCTION vii

CHAPTER 1
KIT-HAN-NE: THE EARLY YEARS 1

CHAPTER 2
THE ENGLISH CONNECTION 7

CHAPTER 3
KIT-HAN-NE WAR CHIEFS: THE PAINTED TERROR ... 15

CHAPTER 4
THE BURNING OF FORT GRANVILLE 21

CHAPTER 5
SEPTEMBER 8, 1756: THE ATTACK ON KIT-HAN-NE .. 27

CHAPTER 6
THE SKIRMISH AT BLANKET HILL 33

CHAPTER 7
KIT-HAN-NE: AFTER THE ATTACK and the
END OF THE FRENCH & INDIAN WAR 39

CHAPTER 8
KIT-HAN-NE: REVOLUTIONARY WAR ERA 45

CHAPTER 9
END OF NATIVE INCURSIONS 53

CHAPTER 10
AUTHOR'S THOUGHTS 63

CHRONOLOGICAL TABLE OF EVENTS 69

BIBLIOGRAPHY 73

A TRIBUTE TO ALL OF THOSE PEOPLE OF 250 YEARS AGO WHO PLAYED A PART IN THE HISTORY OF KITTANNING, PENNSYLVANIA

INTRODUCTION

I always had a fascination with history, especially local history. When I was a young boy, my father, Allen Smail, often took me along to search area corn fields for Indian arrowheads. I can show anyone the first point that I found even though it is in a case of hundreds of additional arrowheads. In my pre-teen years, I played with a plastic flintlock (it used caps) and an old leather purse for a hunting bag and a powder horn that my dad made for me. Yes, I loved 18th century history as a boy, too! I remember the disappointment in discovering that Daniel Boone didn't wear a coonskin cap, as portrayed in the television series from the 1960 era.

Of course, as a young boy seeking to learn, many questions would come up concerning those people who created the still-sharpened points. My dad enjoyed talking about the Indians of Kit-Han-Ne (present day Kittanning) and the eventual attack on this village. He said the Indians only fought to protect their lands and exist. These discussions only fueled my desire to gain more knowledge. Unfortunately, information on this period was not an easy thing to find at that time. Yes, books were written, but we had not known about them. Also, there would only be a paragraph or two concerning the French and Indian War period in our school history books. The War for Independence always took precedence. I personally believe that all of our students should be introduced and taught about our local history. Knowledge of our past definitely aids in the understanding of how we as a people have become what we are. And, knowledge of the past can help all to appreciate the sacrifices of so many over those years.

The purpose of this writing has one primary reason— to foster in readers a desire to become acquainted with the history of the Kittanning area. It is my desire for any reader to gain a yearning and continue seeking information in order to "put it all together". These writings are in no way a complete history of 18th century Kittanning, or of the Delaware tribes, the French and English and the other individuals that were later to become the American people. This writing might be considered a "snap shot" of all the varied events that surrounded the details of the times.

As you read the following chapters and other pertinent books on this subject, you must always keep in mind a sad fact of history. That fact stems from possible biased recordings of the era. Each individual recorder of events may have purposely chosen to elaborate on facts or omit various truths that would have a negative impact on their particular issues of importance. This is human nature. Lieutenant Colonel John Armstrong, in his reports to his superiors, reported on certain issues. We will never know the accuracy of his writings. You will read interesting facts about the attack and the results, of which many aspects caused me to ponder. There are no known documents from the native people on the account. Each reader has to complete a visual of the account within his/ her thoughts and weigh the words before coming to any decision on the subject.

The war that would engulf these people of Kit-Han-Ne would become known as the French and Indian War— a war that would witness much brutality from all involved. Cultures would be drastically altered in the years to follow. The natives were caught up in the middle of a great power struggle; one they could not win. Survival was the best they could expect.

The statement "History repeats itself" is often mentioned by historical scholars. It is a statement of truth. When one delves into the depths of the history of Kit-Han-Ne and all the people involved, a truth becomes apparent. The same scenario that happened in the 18th-century-Kittanning time frame has happened time and time again over the years. The people and places will change, but the events remain shockingly constant…those who want and have power and money will take from those who do not. You can see this formula all over the earth, in all countries and with all nationalities and, unfortunately, this way of thinking will continue until a creator finally says enough.

As I stated earlier, this writing is not supposed to be an in depth account of the history of Kittanning. Hopefully, this writing should be a catalyst for individuals to search for more. There are numerous books on the French and Indian War period. Kittanning is mentioned many times and lots of history surrounds the subject. I urge you to take another step and seek out the knowledge of our historical past. It will be time well spent. So let us begin our journey into the early stages of the Kittanning area, its people and the reasons for **"THE ATTACK ON KIT-HAN-NE.**

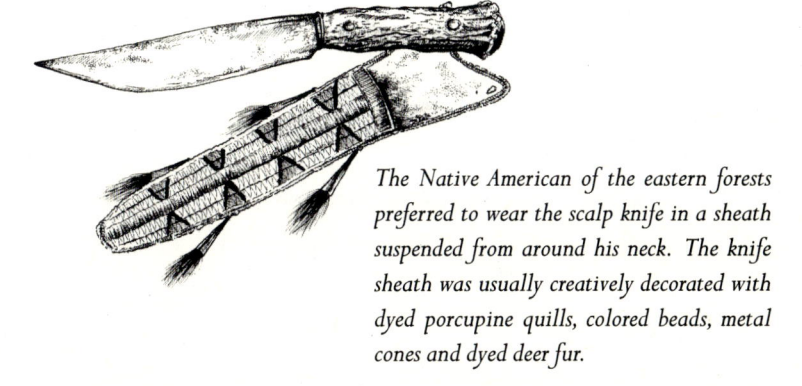

The Native American of the eastern forests preferred to wear the scalp knife in a sheath suspended from around his neck. The knife sheath was usually creatively decorated with dyed porcupine quills, colored beads, metal cones and dyed deer fur.

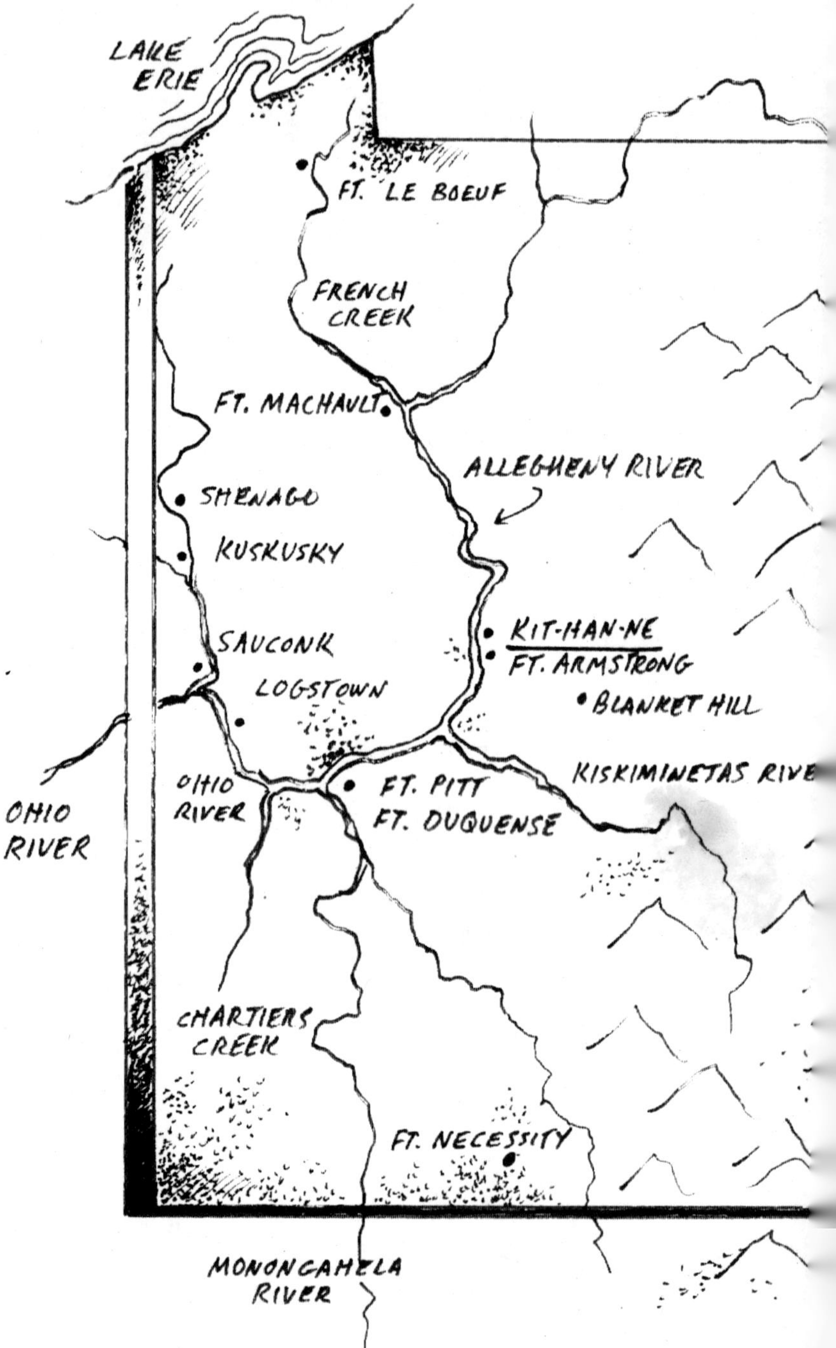

LAKE ERIE
FT. LE BOEUF
FRENCH CREEK
FT. MACHAULT
ALLEGHENY RIVER
SHENAGO
KUSKUSKY
KIT-HAN-NE
FT. ARMSTRONG
SAUCONK
LOGSTOWN
BLANKET HILL
KISKIMINETAS RIVE
OHIO RIVER
FT. PITT
FT. DUQUENSE
OHIO RIVER
CHARTIERS CREEK
FT. NECESSITY
MONONGAHELA RIVER
VIRGINIA

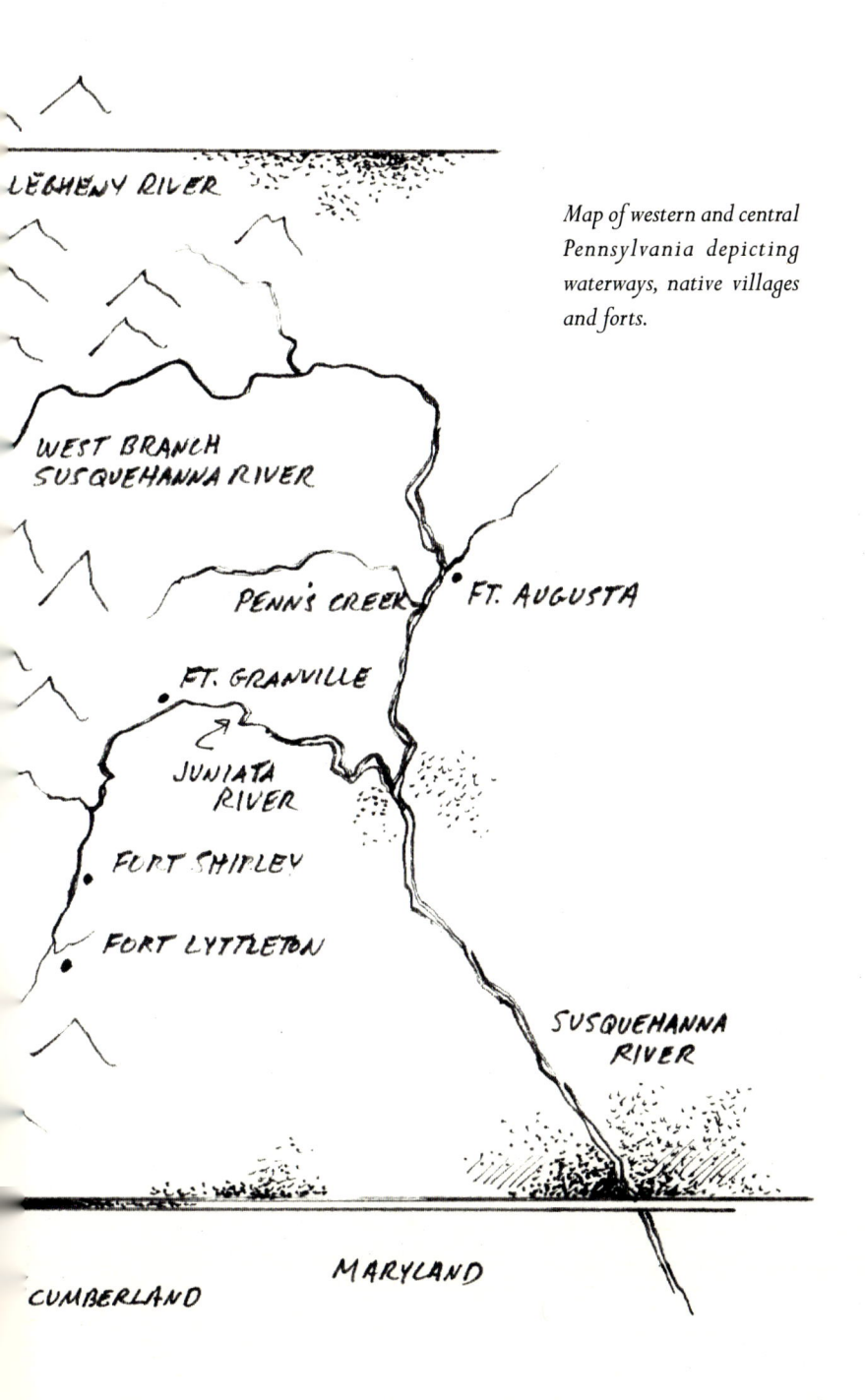

Map of western and central Pennsylvania depicting waterways, native villages and forts.

Kit-Han-Ne War Chief Shingas discussing war strategy with a French soldier in 1755.

CHAPTER 1

KIT-HAN-NE: THE EARLY YEARS

I occasionally spend time in my own little world where I like to ponder the past. I actually yearn to be able to go back in time. I often explore my thoughts and visualize what the area of present day Kittanning would have looked like prior to the inhabitation of man. Picture, if you will, a much shallower, natural flowing and more beautiful Allegheny River winding through the steep Pennsylvania hills. These hills would be covered with huge hardwoods, high pines and hemlocks. Chestnuts would still be a common and valuable tree. Mountain laurel and rhododendron, on the northern slopes, would fill in the lower canopy. Birch and aspens would be standing proud along the flood plain of the great stream. Clear running springs would be spilling from the hills' sides and meandering towards the river. The waters were clean, clear and filled with many species of fish. Wild flowers would be abundant and a common sight. I find it difficult to imagine how quiet those times must have been— so quiet that one could actually hear nature talking to you. Can you visualize walks in the woods without the constant sounds of traffic? Yes, those times would be grandiose!

During my research in preparation for this writing, one fact I discovered is the variance in years for the establishment of Kit-Han-Ne. Historical scholars have a seven year span covered for probable dates of the earliest arrivals of the Delaware Indians. One must remember that the years of the 18th century often failed to have reliable deeds, documents and other records; hence the seven-year spread of possible years for the town's establishment. The years that I have found in my search covered possible dates from 1723 to 1730

ATTACK ON KIT-HAN-NE

for the establishment of Kit-Han-Ne. I personally believe the earlier years are probably the closest to being correct.

Whatever the year, the Turtle and Turkey Clans of the Lenni-Lenape (Delaware) began, with permission from the Iroquoian Six Nations, their westward migration to the western side of the Allegheny Mountain Range. These tribes left their region near the forks of the Susquehanna River to settle among the valleys of the Allegheny and Ohio Rivers of western Pennsylvania. (In the early years the Allegheny and Ohio were considered the same river— the Ohio.) Here, at least some settled and began to build their first town called Kit-Han-Ne. (Kit-Han-Ne is one of several different spellings in the Delaware language.) The name means, "At the great stream" or "At the great river". This is the area of present-day Kittanning, Pennsylvania, which is located in Armstrong County. Other Delaware towns were established along the rivers too. (The Wolf Clan of the Delaware would be migrating at a later date, which is discussed in later chapters.)

I, personally, pondered on Kit-Han-Ne's past prior to the above mentioned migration. I wondered if the Lenni-Lenape (Delaware) possibly had stopped at this same site during an earlier eastern migration. Had their ancestors told them of the area? Another consideration is the possibility that other tribes of years past had settled the area and left signs of their occupancy. There is evidence of unknown Indian habitation from ages past at other sites upstream from the Indian town such as the "Fishbasket" site north of New Bethlehem, Pennsylvania (Clarion County). The last possibility may be simply that the Delaware ventured onto this site, liked what the land had to offer and began to build upon it. These are all speculations; the truth is no one can know the answer to all the reasons the Indians settled at this particular area.

It is known in these early years that white traders had been already frequenting the Kit-Han-Ne town. The natives welcomed traders to the western side of the mountains, but they frowned upon permanent settling. Unfortunately, the Delaware tribes, like so many other tribes, had developed a dependency on the trade goods. This dependency would become one factor towards their eventual demise.

A prominent Delaware chief of Kit-Han-Ne during the early years was a man known as Captain Hill or "Great Hill". In 1731, traders of the area were sending reports to the provincial authorities. In their reports, Captain Hill is mentioned, as well as information on Indian towns such as populations and locations. The traders wrote that about 50 families were living in the Indian town in 1731.

Captain Hill, apparently, was a leader of great respect, for he enjoyed high esteem and held a position comparable to that of a Delaware "King". He may have been guiding migrating natives to Kit-Han-Ne in or around the 1728 time slot. It is known that he was present at grievance meetings in Philadelphia in 1740. I could find no record of his death.

Early in our school years, we are taught about the Quaker William Penn. In the year 1682, Penn sailed from England to his new province, Pennsylvania. William Penn, from all accounts, was an honest and God-fearing man believing in treating all fairly. This belief included the Delaware Indians, many of which lived at that time on the eastern parts of the Pennsylvania Province. Penn treated the Indians in a just and kind manner. The Delaware, in turn, welcomed him with an open heart and open hands.

William Penn decided to follow the Quaker policy of treating the Indians fairly when additional land was in need. Rather than use force and/or deceit, he negotiated with the leaders of the tribe and purchased any land on an agreed upon price. And Penn enacted laws that benefited the Indians. After learning, through complaints from the Delaware leaders, that land speculators would often use liquor to intoxicate Indians in order to cheat them out of land and goods, he passed regulations limiting the sale of liquor to the natives.

Penn, along with his good policies, created a firm and lasting peace. His agreement, called the "Great Treaty", lasted for nearly forty years. This treaty was not broken until 1755, when the Delaware Indians allied themselves with the French during the French and Indian War and attacked the settlers in what became known as

ATTACK ON KIT-HAN-NE

the Penn's Creek Massacre (October 16, 1755). This area is in the general vicinity of present-day Selinsgrove, Pennsylvania in Snyder County.

As we all realize, time moves on; the friend of the Delaware, William Penn, died in July of the year 1718. As to be expected, Penn's sons became heirs to his province. Also, as could be expected, the ways and beliefs of the father would not be carried on by the sons. Many wrongs against the natives would be the result and after a time, revolt would become inevitable.

In 1734 Thomas Penn claimed that he had discovered a treaty dated in 1686 and that the Delaware had been living on lands they did not own. This claim started a scenario to push the natives out and off of these lands. Interestingly enough, the treaty Thomas Penn claimed to have discovered was not the original treaty which conveniently had been lost over the years.

The Delaware leaders, after realizing that their argument over the land and this purported deed was futile, eventually concurred with a new treaty. The infamous "Walking Purchase Treaty" was agreed upon by both parties, as was a date and a starting point. The land, per treaty, would be measured by a one and one-half day walk. Whatever land was covered with this walk in that allotted time span would become the land in question and the matter would be finally closed.

The Delaware leaders, however, did not predict the treachery and deceit of the colonial authorities. The authorities advertised for fast-running athletes. In the ad, whoever covered the longest distance would receive 500 acres of land and monetary gains. Three runners were hired for the task. Also, unbeknown to the Delaware, the authorities blazed a trail through the land and had all brush cleared to make running easier. Imagine their surprise, when the Delaware noticed the brush cleared into a trail! Further imagine their surprise when the walking individuals started running the trail!

The day of the walk proved fruitless for the Indian overseers. The cleared trail and fast-running athletes caused them to protest loudly, but, to no avail. When the "walk" had been completed, the

KITTANNING, PENNSYLVANIA

land measured would be double that which the Indians had anticipated.

Years of petitions, discussions and arguments by the Delaware leaders were in vain. The leaders even petitioned the governor of the province. The results are typical and expected....the Delaware Indians would be leaving. The westward migration of the Wolf Clan of the Delaware Nation began in 1742. Many would be joining their cousins in Kit-Han-Ne.

This migration of the Delaware Indians occurred at a crucial time in Pennsylvania history. The French, too, had been exploring the valleys of the Allegheny and the Ohio. The French were sympathetic to the Delaware people, at least on the surface. The Walking Purchase injustice would be a constant thorn in the side of the Delaware tribe, one that would aid in future decisions during the upcoming war. The French officers reminded the natives often.

One of the next events to be mentioned is of the Celeron Expedition. As previously stated, the country of France was actively seeking the Allegheny and Ohio lands for a time. In 1749, the French led by Captain Celeron de Bienville descended the Allegheny River to bury lead plates at various locations. (The French name for the Allegheny [Ohio] River was "La belle Riviere" which in English means "The Beautiful River".) These lead plates were inscribed with words claiming the lands of the Allegheny-Ohio Rivers for the Crown of France.

Celeron, in the course of his travels, visited Indian towns along his route. His primary intent was to show friendship with the natives, and to gain a trust and alliance. This could help to insure possible allies for any future conflicts with the English.

The French officer reported that Kit-Han-Ne had been abandoned upon his approach; he had sent word ahead to explain to the natives the purpose of his visit, but the Indians retreated into the forest. In his report, Celeron postulated that there were 22 dwellings at the Kit-Han-Ne Indian town. This would, if accurate, have been a decrease from the earlier reports of traders claiming the existence of 50 families in the Indian town.

ATTACK ON KIT-HAN-NE

As you can see, the Indian town of Kit-Han-Ne and its inhabitants were gradually becoming a village and a people of importance to others. The Delaware knew the presence of the French in the valley was not a positive one. The natives, however, appreciated the sympathetic overtone and the goods received from the French. Time would tell how the players and their actions would evolve. Those native leaders of wisdom sensed the probable results of such a presence. Neutrality would prove to be impossible to attain.

The next chapter of the Indian town's history would see another group enter the picture...the English!

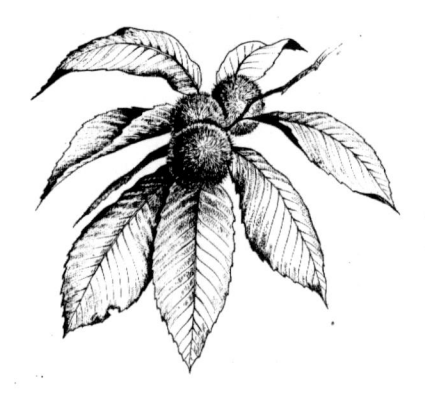

The American Chestnut was a most important and valuable tree in colonial times. The nut of the tree was a food source for both people and wildlife. An introduced blight all but decimated this specie in the early half of the 1900's.

CHAPTER 2

THE ENGLISH CONNECTION

So far, we have learned about the very early years of present-day Kittanning and a time of Delaware migrations into the area, with the establishment of the Indian town of Kit-Han-Ne. We have also ascertained about the entrance of another culture into this colonial period and the western Pennsylvania landscape...the French!

During these early years, the French presence and activities were becoming more and more pronounced. They were exploring the Allegheny and Ohio watersheds, including their tributaries. The French were also sending emissaries into the Indian towns. This, of course, was a strategy to strengthen bonds and, hopefully, ensure alliances for any future conflicts. As we have seen in the last chapter, lead plates were buried at strategic sites, claiming the lands for France. These above mentioned facts and the building of forts along the waterways were not going unnoticed!

Another element, leading to the attack of Kit-Han-Ne, was beginning to make its presence known in the area of western Pennsylvania...enter the English (the pre-American people of the Pennsylvania and Virginia Provinces)!

Governor Dinwiddie, of the Virginia Province, upon hearing of these French activities, saw a need for prompt action in regards to the rights of the English and the Ohio Company. The Ohio Company (formed in 1748) was organized of men from the Virginia Province for the sole purpose of profiting from land speculation. Do you remember hearing of such activities earlier? These same lands, however, were in dispute with the Pennsylvania Province.

Virginia believed the ownership of the 200,000 acres of land located in what is now western Pennsylvania had been determined

ATTACK ON KIT-HAN-NE

through an agreement with the northern Iroquois tribes. Dinwiddie believed the Lancaster Treaty of 1744 had extinguished all rights of these lands from the Iroquois, thus granting ownership of the Ohio valley to the Virginians. (In fact, this above mentioned and disputed land area, and the lands that included Kittanning, would not become white man's property until the signing of the Treaty of Fort Stanwix in 1768.)

Governor Dinwiddie's resolve to protest this French invasion failed with his first attempt. The governor needed someone with qualities that provided the moral and physical stamina for such a dangerous mission. He then appointed a young man of 21 years of age to go the French and demand their expulsion from their (Virginia) lands. The name of this man is known by all grade school students— none other than George Washington, later to become the first president of the United States. Washington's order was to travel north through the wilderness of the Ohio-Allegheny River, a distance of some 500 miles. He was to deliver the grievance to the French leadership against their encroachment into "Virginia" lands. After much planning, Washington began his trek north during the fall of 1753.

The arduous journey at a time of year when Pennsylvania's weather can become harsh attests just how important these actions were to the authorities of Virginia. Mr. Washington, during this trip, met with various native leaders including a well-known Delaware chief named Shingas. (See chapter 3.) Although I have found no positive indications of such, Washington and his men may have, at sometime, stopped at Kit-Han-Ne to meet with the chiefs there.

On December 4th, 1753 the Washington party arrived at Venango (present-day Franklin, Pennsylvania, in Venango County). The French treated him with the utmost respect, even though the message delivered was a protest against their occupation in the Allegheny Valley. The French, on the other hand, let it be plainly known that they (the French) were determined to use every means possible to retain the possession of this disputed territory. This was the site of Fort Machault.

Washington, after this failure of cooperation, proceeded up the headwaters of French Creek (a tributary of the Allegheny) to Fort Le Boeuf (present-day Waterford, Pennsylvania, in Erie County) only to hear more of the same from the French officers there. Then began the long, dangerous return journey to Virginia with the details to Governor Dinwiddie. Washington, in fact, nearly lost his life on more than one occasion during this and later trips to the north.

On January 16th, 1754, Washington delivered the French responses and the results were predictable. Troops would be sent north to force compliance of Virginia's orders. In February 1754 Dinwiddie commissioned a force to the forks of the Ohio (present-day Pittsburgh) to build a fort for an offensive against the French. By April the construction of this fort would be stopped by a constituency of French and Canadian soldiers with a number of Indian allies. This superior force demanded immediate surrender. The construction ceased and the force surrendered. The French and Indian War had officially started although no shots were fired. The French then proceeded to build Fort Duquesne at this site, where the Allegheny and Monongahela Rivers meet to become the Ohio River.

Word reached Dinwiddie, and to counter this surrender and act of war, Washington and 150 men, were again en route to the valleys of the Ohio. This objective began in May of 1754. Washington, through Indian scouts, learned of a small French force near an area of present-day Fayette County, Pennsylvania, known as the Great Meadows. Washington engaged a group of Indian allies, and on May 28, 1754, after much council, they agreed to unite against the French force. The combined force of Washington's men and Seneca Chief Tanacharison's (Half-King) Indians attacked the French in a battle that lasted about 15 minutes. The French were soundly defeated. The commander of the French was M. de Jumonville. He, too, was killed at this battle.

The first shots of the French and Indian War had been fired. The war had begun. There would be no turning back from this point, for blood had been shed!

ATTACK ON KIT-HAN-NE

At the Great Meadows, Washington had a fort of palisades quickly erected in anticipation of a French response. This structure was called Fort Necessity because it was built out of necessity. This site would become the next scene of actual battle between the two forces.

Reinforcements began arriving at the fort in preparation of a strategic attack on the French fort, Fort Duquesne. At this same time a stronger force of French and Indians left the fort on June 28, 1754, to strike back at Washington. The French commander was M. De Villiers and he was the half-brother of Jumonville killed in Washington's earlier attack.

The French attacked Washington's forces at Fort Necessity despite a torrential rainfall. By evening, due to the overpowering numbers of the French, the fort was surrendered. Washington, surprisingly, was permitted to surrender with all the honors of war! However, he did sign a paper that, written in the French language, unbeknownst to him, was an admission of guilt to the "assassination" of Jumonville.

The news of Washington's surrender at Fort Necessity sent out an alarm throughout the colonies and also among the local British authorities. England, learning of the surrender, fully understood what the French intentions were. They were willing to take action to remove the French from the valuable lands of the Allegheny and Ohio Rivers. Force would be required!

In England, General Edward Braddock began to plan and prepare troops to send to the colonies to resist the French aggressions. The general was soon to become deeply aware of the problems and dangers of the wild forests of Pennsylvania.

Braddock was an arrogant officer. Benjamin Franklin warned him of Indian ambushes and capabilities. The general's reply, according to Franklin's autobiography, was, "These savages may indeed be a formidable enemy to your raw American militia, but upon the King's regular and disciplined troops, sir, it is impossible that they should make any impression."

KITTANNING, PENNSYLVANIA

The general's orders were to take the war to the French at Fort Duquesne and claim the site for England. The march headed for present-day Pittsburgh began in the spring of 1755. The journey took Braddock's army across the rugged terrain of the Pennsylvania mountain range. The army, in typical English grandeur, crossed the Monongahela River on July 9th at around 2:00 in the afternoon. Drums and fifes were playing and the flag of England danced in the breeze. The music was soon to change from drums and fifes to the sounds of musket fire and whooping natives out to kill.

After Braddock's army crossed the river onto the northern embankment, the encounter with the French and Indian force was soon forthcoming. Shots were fired and, after a brief pause by the Indians due to the death of the French leader, the fight resumed in earnest. The Indians began to flank the King's troops and, in typical native fashion, hurled blood-curdling screams and well placed shots from the forest concealment, wreaking havoc on the soldiers. This psychological strategy unnerved the troops into a frenzy. The ranks

The British "Brown Bess" musket shot a .75 caliber lead ball. Armed with a 14-inch bayonet, the "Bess" was a formidable and lethal weapon.

ATTACK ON KIT-HAN-NE

were falling apart as the panic became more pronounced. George Washington had two horses shot out from under him and had four musket balls pass through the material of his uniform. He, unbelievably, escaped harm! (The legendary Daniel Boone served as a wagoner during the battle.)

The fracas continued and the panic increased to a point that troops actually abandoned their weapons while in a headlong flight to get back across the river. General Braddock himself was mortally wounded and died a few days later. Braddock began the fight with 1200 British troops and additional provincial troops to total approximately 1460 troops under his command; but, when the shooting had stopped, approximately 900 or so were dead or dying. Others were captured, only to be tortured, at Fort Duquesne. This battle was to be the most crushing defeat ever administered to the British army on American soil. Had the French and Indian force pursued the retreating British army, a complete annihilation would have been the result. Indian mentality was such that when they felt they had done enough in battle they would simply quit to begin a plunder and scalping session. Reports claim there were 43 French and Canadians killed or wounded and 27 Indians killed or wounded.

The defeat of the British army in southwestern Pennsylvania would prove to be detrimental to the future of many undecided natives of the Kit-Han-Ne town. The soon-to-be-made decisions would quickly see the effect of Braddock's defeat across the eastern side of the mountain range…Delaware war parties!

Kit-Han-Ne War Chief Captain Jacobs would have resembled the native illustrated here. The huge feather bonnet was used by the natives of the western states. Eastern warriors preferred little clothing when fighting.

CHAPTER 3

KIT-HAN-NE WAR CHIEFS: THE PAINTED TERROR

> NOTICE IS HEREBY GIVEN, THAT THE SUM OF SEVEN HUNDRED PIECES OF EIGHT IS RAISED BY SUBSCRIPTION AMONG THE INHABITANTS OF THE CITY OF PHILADELPHIA, AND NOW OFFERED WITH THE APPROBATION OF HIS HONOUR THE GOVERNOR, AS A REWARD FOR ANY PERSON OR PERSONS WHO SHALL BRING INTO THIS CITY THE HEADS OF SHINGAS AND CAPTAIN JACOBS, CHIEFS OF THE DELAWARE INDIAN NATION; OR THREE HUNDRED AND FIFTY PIECES OF EIGHT FOR EACH...
>
> Virginia followed suit with an offer of "AN HUNDRED PISTOLES" for the "HEADS OF KING SHINGAS AND CAPTAIN JACOBS..." or "FIFTY PISTOLES FOR EACH...."

The incredible defeat of the English army, under the command of General Edward Braddock, had a most desirable effect on the Delaware and Shawnee of Kit-Han-Ne. That victory for the French and their Indian allies was just what the French needed to have the Kit-Han-Ne Indians commit to their cause. The French needed these natives to strike terror into the heart of the provinces and also, to aid them in fighting the English.

Prior to the above mentioned defeat, the Kit-Han-Ne Delawares were reluctant to enter into the worsening fray. The native

ATTACK ON KIT-HAN-NE

leaders realized their neutrality could not last as the two great armies strengthened and continued preparing for further war. It is true the French treated them much more favorably than the English with trade goods and presents. The Indians needed these "goods", since they had, unfortunately, become dependent on many of the white man's "luxuries" of which they had no means to produce themselves. These items included important things of the day, such as lead, black powder, firearms, firearm repair work, musket balls, gun parts and cloth for clothing.

 The Delaware basically wanted to continue all trade, but they also wanted all English colonists and the French to eventually leave their valleys and keep all permanent settlements on the eastern side of the Pennsylvania mountain range. One must remember that throughout the many years of future conflicts, the Delaware never wavered on these demands! If indeed they were to become involved with this fracas, they, of course, wanted to be on the winning team too. Obviously, the natives wished to be where their people would benefit the most at the close of the war. The "Walking Purchase" memories would also play an integral part in the decision-making process. Remember that injustice of almost twenty years ago was still a subject of anger to the native population of Kit-Han-Ne. Another aspect that helped with the decision to go to war against the English was the haughty words used by General Braddock to Chief Shingas. The native leader pleaded with the general not to rob the Delaware of their lands. Braddock replied that the "English should inhabit and inherit land and that no savage should inherit the land." This, of course, enraged the Indians.

 Their observations, at this time, saw the French as a stronger force than the English, especially after Braddock's defeat. Receiving better treatment from the French, the memories of the Walking Purchase Treaty, and Braddock's attitude all played major parts in the decision for the Kit-Han-Ne Indians to join the French alliance. The war was about to become brutal! The "painted terror" was heading east!

....

KITTANNING, PENNSYLVANIA

One primary chief of Kit-Han-Ne was Captain Jacobs. He "took up the hatchet" against the English and those people of Pennsylvania and Virginia after Braddock's defeat. Captain Jacobs once lived near present-day Lewistown, Pennsylvania (Mifflin County) where he sold lands to a Colonel Buchanan. The Colonel said that the Delaware reminded him of a burly German settler living in Cumberland County who was named Jacob. The name caught on, and the English and colonists of that time referred to the chief as Captain Jacobs.

The chief also once lived near present-day Mount Pleasant, Pennsylvania (Westmoreland County), the area known as Jacobs Cabin. However, by the mid-18th century Jacobs resided in his principal residence of Kit-Han-Ne.

It was from this Indian town that Captain Jacobs and Shingas led many a bloody incursion into the eastern frontiers of Pennsylvania, Maryland and Virginia. Jacobs was the Delaware leader of the Indian attack and burning of Fort Granville. (More on this attack will be in the next chapter.)

A very sad fact of Captain Jacobs' past is there are so few records about him in existence. His biography is short. I would love to have been able to meet the man in times of peace. I have to admit that much of my fascination about him stems from the lack of information on his life prior to the war. In fact, there isn't much known about him during the war. Obviously, he was a very brave and courageous man, one willing to sacrifice his life for his beliefs. The fact worsens because no matter how much knowledge I crave, I will not be able to further satisfy my curiosity because of the lack of information. He will, forever, be a mystery to me.

There were numerous attacks committed by Captain Jacobs and his Delaware warriors. We can never know every incident that he personally was involved in, but the list of incursions into the frontier settlements during this war is a long one.

Captain Jacobs was reportedly killed at least twice prior to the attack on Kit-Han-Ne. One report stated that he was killed in Janu-

ATTACK ON KIT-HAN-NE

ary 1756 in Northampton County. The second report related that he was killed in Cumberland County in April of the same year.

The other war chief who resided at Kit-Han-Ne during this war of the empires was a man named Shingas. He belonged to the Turkey Clan of the Delaware Nation. He, like Captain Jacobs, was a ruthless warrior in battle. His list of bloody incursions is also a long one.

Moravian missionary John Heckewelder, spent many years amidst the Delaware. He knew Shingas personally. He reported that Shingas wasn't a real tall man, but his savage prowess was never exceeded by anyone. Heckewelder also made note that Shingas treated prisoners kindly.

Shingas became "King of the Delawares" in 1752. This "kingship" title, however, was a title bestowed in honor only. The "official" king had to be chosen by warriors of the Turtle Clan. The head chief was regarded as "king" of the three Delaware clans: the Wolf Clan, the Turkey Clan and the Turtle Clan. Shingas was called King Shingas by many.

The Delaware chief was one of the native leaders who met with George Washington at present-day McKees Rocks, Pennsylvania in 1753. His name can be found in numerous records in association with treaty negotiations and signings, peace talks and other pertinent meetings.

During the French and Indian War and after Braddock's defeat, Shingas allied himself with the French. In the fall of 1755, he and Captain Jacobs set in motion the bloody raids on the settlements of the eastern frontier. He was responsible for the burning of Fort McCord (in present-day Franklin County). The Pennsylvania province offered rewards for both Shingas' and Captain Jacobs' scalps. He was known as "Shingas the Terrible" by many along the frontier, as well as the colonial authorities.

Shingas chose to take up arms against the English again during Pontiac's War. He made this decision after realizing that the whites could not be trusted to uphold their agreements made in 1758 after the French deserted Fort Pitt. He participated in the siege of Fort

Pitt in July 1763. And he may have been involved at the Battle of Bushy Run in present-day Westmoreland County.

Like the previous chief, I would have enjoyed discussing life with Shingas albeit in times of peace. From the numerous quotes attributed to him, it appears that he was a man of wisdom, unfortunate to be caught up within the great power struggles of the 18th century. He was a man of high esteem both in peace and at war. Shingas may have passed on during the winter of 1763-1764.

CHAPTER 4

THE BURNING OF FORT GRANVILLE

The summer of 1756 continued to witness the "savage fury" unleashed on the frontiers of the Pennsylvania, Maryland and Virginia Provinces. These Indians were at war and their attacks caused many people of the frontier to flee, die or be taken into captivity. Homes and settlements were plundered and burned; livestock was killed or run off and crops destroyed. Some captured individuals were sold or traded to the French and others were adopted into the tribe. Still others were sentenced to die a tortuous and cruel death.

The Delaware leaders were confident in their abilities to conduct war. The proof of this confidence could easily be observed along the frontier settlements and in the terror-stricken faces of the victims who left their homes with little more than the clothes on their back. The tear-stained cheeks and wide, delusional eyes spoke volumes to those of the more inhabited towns of the East.

Braddock made the fatal mistake of believing the "savages" were not able to commit to a disciplined war. In his mind, only the English had the essential mental qualities and training. His arrogance was buried along with his body and those hundreds killed along with his defeat! The natives proved time and time again they had the ability to plan and carry out strategic battles and come out on top!

In retrospect, there were other elements added to the times that aggravated the native problems. For instance, on April 8, 1756, the Pennsylvania leadership declared war on the Delaware and Shawnee tribes. With this declaration of war, a new and controversial law was also enacted. This new law was called the "Scalp Act." This act offered monetary bounties to be paid for Indian prisoners or scalps. Variations in the amounts depended on the sex and/or age of the individual Indians. Men or scalps of men over twelve years of age brought the highest amounts of monetary gains. Women and natives under twelve years of age brought less. As to be expected, this act further infuriated the natives and forced otherwise undecided Indians to take up arms against the province.

In the latter part of July 1756, Kit-Han-Ne War Chief Captain Jacobs began the attack on Fort Granville, a provincial fort of Pennsylvania. This fort was located along the Juniata River near present-day Lewistown, Pennsylvania (Mifflin County). He was accompanied by French officer Captain Coulon de Villiers (the same officer that defeated George Washington at Fort Necessity in 1754). French reports claim a total of 23 French and 32 Indians participated in the attack.

Fort Granville was under the command of Captain Edward Ward. Around July 22, 1756, possibly around 60 native warriors were, reportedly, observed lurking around the perimeters of the fort. Later, a challenge to fight was proposed to those in the fort. The challenge was denied by Ward due to the perceived weakness of the colonial force. The Indians, for reasons only known to them, eventually divided their force and went elsewhere to wreak havoc.

One of the divided forces may have retreated to wait for French forces, or possibly just to wait in the shadows and spy on the actions of the fort's command, but this is only speculation on my part. It must be remembered that a tactic often used by natives was to allow individual warriors to be seen disappearing into the shadows and foliage, only to again appear at other locations, giving the impression of higher numbers. I believe this type of psychological warfare may have been used at the site of Fort Granville. The other force was believed to have made attacks elsewhere.

Circa July 30, 1756, Captain Edward Ward left command of the fort to the lesser-ranked Lieutenant Edward Armstrong. (This man was the brother of Colonel John Armstrong who later would be leading the attack on Kit-Han-Ne.) Captain Ward then proceeded with a detachment to help guard settlers harvesting their crops.

Apparently he deemed the situation safe enough to warrant the risk; after all, there had not been any Indians seen for a week.

Shortly after Ward's departure, the fort was surrounded by a hostile force of French and Indians that immediately attacked and besieged the fort. The attackers were having little impact on the inhabitants of the fort because of the structural strength of the logs. However, the Indians, by way of a deep ravine, managed to creep to within twelve or fifteen yards of the fort. The natives used burning pine knots and continued throwing them at the structure until fire finally kindled and spread.

Armstrong, with others, tried to extinguish the fire, but he was mortally wounded. As the hole burned wider, another private was killed and several others wounded. The battle for the fort was beginning to succumb to the actions of the French and the Indians. The fort was about to fall!

An Indian, probably Captain Jacobs, demanded surrender and offered to spare the lives of those inside the fort. A corporal named John Turner decided to open the gates of the fort. The war-whooping and painted warriors entered, and began taking prisoners and gathering plunder. A total of 22 men, three women and some children (including the famous Girty boys of Revolutionary War fame) were forced into carrying plunder and began the treacherous trip across the mountains to Kit-Han-Ne. Captain Jacobs and his warriors continued to burn the fort to the ground.

Upon their arrival at the Indian town, the prisoners were treated cruelly by their captors, as was their custom when returning from battle. John Turner, after native council, was elected to be tortured to death for past deeds. He was said to have killed his comrade Simon Girty, Sr., in order to marry Girty's wife. His torture lasted roughly three hours before a tomahawk to the skull ended his torment.

Colonial confidence was at an all-time low after the attack and burning of Fort Granville. Fort Shirley (present-day Shirleysburg, Pennsylvania, Huntington County) and others were evacuated after the defeat of Fort Granville. Captain Jacobs and his warriors were

ATTACK ON KIT-HAN-NE

further elated over the results. Jacobs made the statement, "I can take any fort that will catch fire and I will make peace with the English when they teach me to make gun powder."

Some prisoners were taken to Fort Duquesne (present-day Pittsburgh, Allegheny County). While at the fort, Captain Jacobs reportedly traded Lieutenant Armstrong's boots with a French officer for a new powder horn and a pouch.

In early October, two prisoners captured at Fort Granville managed to escape and return to Fort Lyttleton (present-day Fort Littleton, Fulton County, Pennsylvania).

Many, many incursions happened from the Penns Creek Massacre of October 1755 to late July of 1756. There are numerous accounts recorded about these attacks. These are listed in many books written about the French and Indian War. The burning and defeat of Fort Granville, however, is reported here because of the effects it had on the province, the response of Colonel John Armstrong (Edward Armstrong's brother) and how the scenario eventually lead to the attack on the natives' soil.

Many variations of the tomahawk appeared over the years of the 18th century. The "hawk" was used both as an offensive and defensive weapon. The weapon was also used as a tool for jobs such as cutting firewood.

Lieutenant Colonel John Armstrong,
Pennsylvania Provincial Officer of the Pennsylvania 2nd Battalion.

CHAPTER 5

SEPTEMBER 8, 1756...
THE ATTACK ON KIT-HAN-NE

In the last days of summer in the year 1756, Kittanning looked much different than the town does today—an obvious fact. The structure of the town of Kit-Han-Ne was about to see a rapid change in its appearance and character. The attack of the Pennsylvania Provincial troops was soon to come.

These same observations of change could be said of much of the eastern frontier too. Many settlements consisting of log cabins with barns were burned, leaving only smoldering and charred debris on the ground. A few frontier forts had been burned also. Crops were destroyed. Dead and decaying bodies were an all too common sight at the settlements and yet other bodies were scattered across the Pennsylvania wilderness, many never to be discovered. The war was a brutal one for sure.

The people of the province were making their concerns known to the Pennsylvania authorities. The entire province was engulfed in a reign of fear for their future. After all, few families of the frontier escaped seeing family members or acquaintances affected in some way by the horrors of the Delaware and Shawnee attacks. I believe that one scenario that undoubtedly encouraged the attack on Kit-Han-Ne more than any other was the burning of Fort Granville and the death of Lieutenant Edward Armstrong. As you recall, this man was the brother of Colonel John Armstrong, who would lead the attack. It is true that the burning of the forts Granville and McCord exposed the eastern frontier to more terror from the Indian incursions. Other forts were deemed indefensible and abandoned. Obviously, something needed to be done to bolster the rapidly decaying morale and to curtail the deaths of many.

Colonel John Armstrong of the 2nd Battalion of the Pennsylvania Regiment wrote about these problems and the difficulties of defending the frontier. The response was certain when outgoing Governor Morris and the colonial authorities approved the plans that Armstrong and John Baker devised. Baker was an escaped prisoner from the Indian town and was able to supply important information about the area. Baker reported that over 100 prisoners were located at the village. As previously stated, I am sure the colonel felt a strong need to avenge his brother's death by Captain Jacobs and his warriors.

Armstrong left Fort Shirley on August 30, 1756 and joined an advance party on September 3. At this time the army consisted of 307 men, mostly Scotch Irish from the Cumberland Valley (southeastern Pennsylvania). One report stated that Armstrong may have had a numerical superiority over the natives by a 3-1 margin. The march towards Kit-Han-Ne had begun. The distance along much of the old Kittanning Indian Trail was approximately 126 miles.

As the distance to Kit-Han-Ne shortened, Armstrong elected to keep sending scouts ahead to search for native activity or evidence of a possible ambush. The importance of these scouts became evident when, approximately six miles from the Indian town, the scouts from Armstrong's command discovered a fire encircled by three or four Indians. This discovery was around 10:00 in the evening of September 7, 1756. The colonel, for fear of alerting the town, stationed Lieutenant James Hogg and twelve men behind with orders to attack these Indians at the break of dawn. (Details on the attack of the Indians at the fire are in Chapter 6.)

The remainder of the force detoured around the site and proceeded on toward Kit-Han-Ne. The morning sunrise would soon illuminate the flood plain where the Indian town of Kit-Han-Ne was situated. Everything seemed to be normal; the native activities appeared to be the same as the day before. However, this calm morning— the morning of September 8, 1756— was soon to be interrupted by a barrage of musket balls, smoke, fire and bloodshed.

Armstrong's Pennsylvania Provincial soldiers arrived near the Indian town very early in the morning. The colonel's plan was to position detachments to various areas of the forests around Kit-Han-Ne. He wanted his troops to surround as much of the town as possible before dawn. He retained a large number of troops with him, promising not to begin the attack for about twenty minutes. The time should be ample enough for the detachments to get into the positions assigned to them.

However, prior to the orders for the encirclement of the town, an Indian whistled during the very early hours in a very singular manner. The troops immediately crouched down, unsure of what they heard. John Baker, the escaped prisoner, explained to the colonel that the whistle was a signal by a young Indian fellow to his squaw after his dance. Immediately, small fires were lit in the cornfield. Baker explained that the fires were built to repel gnats.

At the end of the allotted time, the order was directed and the attack began with men moving into the cornfields. Others headed towards the Indian houses. Captain Jacobs, upon hearing of the attack in progress, immediately shouted the war-whoop. The Indian women and children were ordered to head into the forest. An English prisoner later quoted Jacobs who announced, "The white men were at last come; they (the Delaware) would then soon have scalps enough."

The soldiers passed through the fields, taking aim and firing as ordered. With the confusion of the sudden surprise, the Delaware and Shawnee offered only occasional shots. Some shots came from across the western side of the river. (Chief Shingas was living on the west side.) After the initial chaos, a good deal of shooting apparently came from Captain Jacobs' house. Provincial troops firing at the house found that their shots were ineffectual because the logs barricaded those inside. The Indians used portholes cut into the logs through which to shoot, thus offering smaller targets. This tactic caused the death and wounding of some of Armstrong's men.

ATTACK ON KIT-HAN-NE

Armstrong later reported that Captain Jacobs and others from within the confines of his house seldom missed hitting the soldiers whenever any of them offered a clear shot. (A French officer, De Normanville and a few other Frenchmen may have aided the Delaware during the attack.)

The colonel ordered the house to be set on fire. He was wounded in the shoulder while moving about, giving orders. The Indians were told to surrender themselves as prisoners. One voice from the house (probably the chief) demanded that he was a man and would not be a prisoner! The soldier responded, warning him that he would be burned. The Delaware replied that he did not care and that he would kill four or five before he was.

Through great difficulty and luck, one soldier managed to get to the house, start a fire and return to the force— and not be shot. In one report, Jacobs supposedly exclaimed, "I eat fire!" in response to the threat of being burned.

As the fire grew in intensity, one Indian was heard singing his death song to show all that he was not afraid to die. A female began to cry, but was severely rebuked by the men. Shortly thereafter, two men and one woman leaped from the burning building when the fire became too hot. They attempted to run towards the cornfield, but were shot down. It was thought that Captain Jacobs tumbled himself through a garret or cock-loft window and was shot. Escaped prisoners claimed that the man was Jacobs after identifying a powder horn and pouch for which he recently traded boots. The chief had traded Lieutenant Edward Armstrong's boots (from the Fort Granville battle) to a French officer while at Fort Duquesne. Prisoners also claimed they recognized the scalps of Jacobs, his wife and one lad known as the King's Son.

Captain Hugh Mercer was wounded in the arm during the battle and was taken up on the hill. Armstrong, too, went to this site to have his wound tied in order to control the bleeding. He and other officers recognized the fact that Indians from across the river were rallying and beginning to cross the waterway. They feared that the natives were attempting to surround the troops. The colonel wouldn't consent to a retreat until more houses were in flames. According to his report, he believed that close to thirty houses were set afire during the attack.

As the fires spread, explosions from ammunition igniting in the flames could be heard. One house, possibly Captain Jacobs' house, contained kegs of gun powder that detonated with such a force, the blast was said to have been heard at Fort Duquesne nearly 40 miles away. A leg and thigh of an adult along with a young child were seen blown into the air into the adjacent corn field. Prisoners claimed that they heard Indians say that there was enough arms and ammunition for a ten year war with the English. French goods were also destroyed in the fires.

Officers were able to learn valuable intelligence from escaped prisoners. They were informed that two bateaux of French and Delaware were to join Captain Jacobs later on this very day of the attack; they were to organize and set out to attack Fort Shirley the next day. The escaped prisoners told them that about 24 natives were commissioned to possibly obtain meat or spy on the fort! The soldiers realized at this time that the fate of Lieutenant Hogg and his men would be in peril if indeed this was the same band of Indians. It was decided to gather the wounded and retreat, for this reason and the possibility of being surrounded. The original intent was to destroy all the fields of corn to further dampen the natives' desire for war. This act did not happen.

Due to the apprehension of being counterattacked by the natives, it became difficult to keep the men together. These fears were heightened when a few warriors fired upon the retreating force. One soldier was shot through both ankles. Some of the men became lost as the journey proceeded east, including Captain Mercer and four of the escaped prisoners.

The main force of soldiers arrived near the site of the Indian fire and met up with a few deserters from the morning Kit-Han-Ne attack. These men gave an account of the skirmish. They proclaimed there were more Indians at the fire than the scouts had originally reported. The lieutenant and other soldiers had been killed—

others fled in terror! (See chapter 6 for a complete account of this battle and the aftermath.)

The return journey heading for the safety of the forts gathered momentum. There was fear that avenging natives could appear at any moment and at anywhere! There were, however, few natives seen after the initial retreat began. Those natives that were spotted were sporadic. The bulk of the troops returned to Fort Lyttleton on the day of September 14th. Some of the missing reportedly gathered at other forts along the frontier, among them Fort Augusta and Fort Cumberland.

Upon his arrival, Colonel John Armstrong wrote of 17 killed, 13 wounded and 19 missing from his army. He had returned with four or five Indian scalps and seven prisoners. Of the 100 or so white prisoners at the Indian town, most had not been rescued or had escaped. (More details of the battle's aftermath appear in Chapter 7.)

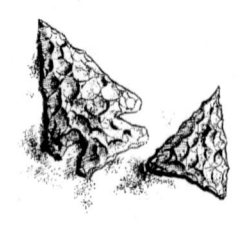

CHAPTER 6

THE SKIRMISH AT BLANKET HILL

AUTHOR'S NOTE: As we read in the last chapter, Colonel John Armstrong, prior to his advance on Kit-Han-Ne, left thirteen men behind to attack the Indians at the fire site. Parts of the following will be viewed as a repeat from the last chapter. The repeated information is important since there is a direct correlation between the Blanket Hill skirmish and the attack on the Indian town.

BLANKET HILL

The approach towards Kit-Han-Ne along the Kittanning Indian Trail could easily become a place for ambush and death. For this reason, Colonel John Armstrong repeatedly sent scouts ahead of the forward advance in search of any Indian activity. The colonel probably couldn't believe his luck had persisted through all these miles since this group left Fort Shirley. To march over 300 men approximately 120 miles towards the Kit-Han-Ne without any Indian sightings or ambush was truly remarkable. I can only imagine the apprehension these men experienced as the distance to the town continually shortened by the hour. Each man, most likely, silently prayed and fought emotions of fear in the best way they could.

Around ten o'clock in the evening of September 7, 1756, approximately six miles from the Indian town, two scouts reported to the colonel of a fire up ahead. They cautioned him about the presence of three or four Indians around the fire.

33

ATTACK ON KIT-HAN-NE

Bronze marker, set in stone, located at Blanket Hill along U.S. 422. Photo by Ruthie Smail

Colonel Armstrong, not wanting any of the natives to escape from this site to forewarn the town, left Lieutenant James Hogg and twelve men behind with orders to attack the Indians at the fire at the break of day. The horses and baggage were left behind too. This was done to further lessen any chance of discovery as the soldiers approached the town. These thirteen men settled in among the forest depths and waited for dawn. The remaining force detoured around the area, hoping to avoid detection.

The hours crept incredibly slowly as the men waited anxiously to have their objective completed. I am sure they pondered what the outcome of the morning would be for them, as well as the troops destined to attack the town. I suspect some may have actually felt a sense of gladness since they wouldn't be part of the primary goal of attacking Kit-Han-Ne.

With the break of dawn, Hogg ordered the attack to commence. As the grays of dawn began to slowly express the forest's colors, the troops inched closer to the Indians. I suspect they were anticipating a quick victory. They were feeling rather confident; af-

KITTANNING, PENNSYLVANIA

ter all, they believed they had superiority in numbers against the Indians. They also had the element of surprise on their side. From a strategic standpoint, both of those positives should lead to an easy and decisive win over the enemy.

After the troops had fallen into position, one of the natives walked near the concealed soldiers. Shots permeated the stillness of the September morning, but the native escaped unharmed. The surprise attack, it is believed, killed or mortally wounded three of the Indians. The next seconds saw more Indians running from their stacked muskets only to return and gather them up before the soldiers could rush them. The result was a brisk counterattack. Unfortunately, this scenario of the battle was beginning to go very wrong for the troops.

As you remember, the scouts claimed there were but three or four natives at the fire. With musket balls flying all about, a stark reality soon was realized....a larger group of war-whooping and angry Delawares were in their midst. It is not known if there were more Indians lying about the fire than viewed by the scouts or if additional Delaware arrived throughout the night. Prisoners that escaped with the Armstrong troops claimed that around 25 Indians were sent out to obtain meat. A company of 150 French and Delaware were scheduled to arrive at Kit-Han-Ne later on the same day of the attack. Other prisoner reports stated that a group of warriors were headed out for more raids, possibly on Fort Shirley as well.

The attack quickly turned against Hogg and his men. The lieutenant was wounded twice. Several of his men were killed and two were wounded.

The Pennsylvania Historical & Museum Commission erected this historical marker at Blanket Hill. The actual battle occurred southeast of the markers. Photo by Ruthie Smail

ATTACK ON KIT-HAN-NE

The remaining men, upon seeing all of these things happening, fled in terror! The wounded Lieutenant took cover in the brush in hopes that the Indians would not locate him. He also hoped that the returning troops from Kit-Han-Ne would be able to find him before any Delaware warrior did.

The troops heading towards the Indian town were having some desertion problems too. Several of the returning deserters from Kit-Han-Ne located Lieutenant Hogg. The wounded officer was lifted onto a horse. They were just beginning their journey out of this dangerous area when four Delaware warriors appeared. The deserters panicked again. Hogg urged them to stay and fight but to no avail. They attempted to flee, but the Indians pursued and killed one of these men and wounded the lieutenant for the third time. The remaining soldiers were able to elude the Indians. Hogg, using the horse to flee, died of his wounds a few hours later.

Well into the day of September 8, 1756, Armstrong's retreating force began to find their way back to the vicinity of the fire site only to learn of additional casualties. Armstrong questioned some deserters about what had happened. They described the Indians' fighting abilities and how the men, out of fear, became nervous and panicky. Their primary concern was survival; so they deserted, leaving behind "a considerable loss of horses and baggage."

The area of this skirmish and the aftermath became known as "Blanket Hill". Troop blankets were left there in the forest as Indians were seen rallying for additional attacks. Any present-day traveler of US Route 422 will not see any village sign along the highway. However, if looking carefully, he or she will notice an historical marker briefly summarizing the Blanket Hill story. Titled "Blanket Hill," the blue and yellow historical marker states: "So named from the blankets left here by the Armstrong expedition after destroying Kittanning. Here also was a stopping point of the troops en route to attack the Indians Sept. 7, 1756."

There is also a bronze marker set in stone. On it is inscribed: "Here Colonel Armstrong, with about 300 frontiersmen from Cumberland County, stopped September 7, 1756, while on his way to attack the Indian town of Kittanning. He left 12 men, commanded by Lieutenant James Hogg, to watch a band of Indians seen at a nearby campfire. The next morning Lieutenant Hogg attacked this band of Indians and was killed with a number of his men. From the many blankets left here by Colonel Armstrong's men, the place received its name." The exact site of the battle is not at the location of these markers.

In the years following the closing chapter of the French and Indian War and during the re-development of the area, local people discovered various relics at the battle site. One such relic was a straight sword with the initials "JH" inscribed on it, assumed to be that of Lieutenant James Hogg. The sword actually was on exhibit at the Centennial Exposition in Philadelphia. I do not know if this sword is currently in existence.

The area of Blanket Hill today is a typical mix of woodlands and farms. In earlier days there was a one-room school and a post office among small businesses and farms. Phillip Dunmire (my great, great, great grandfather) acquired the land where the battle was fought. I have walked and hunted along the hills and valleys of his property, not realizing just how close I was to the battle site.

Today, I look upon the area as a somewhat sacred site. After all, people lived and fought and died here.

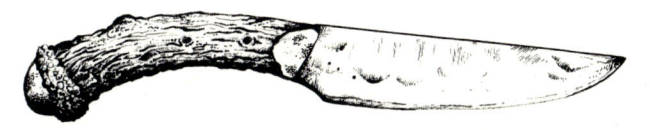

An antler-handle scalp knife

CHAPTER 7

KIT-HAN-NE: AFTER THE ATTACK AND THE END OF THE FRENCH & INDIAN WAR

The Delaware and Shawnee living in Kit-Han-Ne were in a state of disbelief. War Chief Captain Jacobs, his wife, son and others were killed during the attack! A number of native homes were in various stages of burning! Chief Shingas ventured from across the river and surveyed the results of the attack. Anger amongst the natives began to supersede the initial loss and disbelief. How could they have not been prepared and allowed this attack to happen? How did 307 men travel over 120 miles along much of the old Kittanning Indian Trail and not have been detected by some raiding party or a hunting group? The only answer was that of unbelievable luck for the troops and overconfidence of the Delaware people. After all, up to this time, the natives had great success with their raiding parties and no inkling of any organized attack towards their homeland.

Needless to say, Colonel John Armstrong's Provincial Army did not leave the conflict site without men dead and wounded. How many casualties resulted from Armstrong's attack on the Indian town? As stated in chapter 5, the colonel reported that 17 were killed, 13 wounded and 19 missing. It is not known if any of the wounded succumbed to their injuries in the weeks that followed. When one thinks back to the medical profession of the times and the lack of medicinal knowledge, I find it safe to believe that probably a few died over time from their wounds due to infection. Of those listed

ATTACK ON KIT-HAN-NE

as missing, it is known that some managed to return to several frontier forts over time.

Captain Hugh Mercer was persuaded to leave the main troop by some of his men; they claimed there was a shorter route. Four of the escaped prisoners decided to go with this group too. At some point this group came upon the Indians that were believed to be the same natives involved with Lieutenant Hogg's attack. A skirmish was the result, leaving some of Mercer's men killed. The captain and two of his men escaped. Upon seeing a native approaching them, the two men fled with the native in pursuit, but Mercer concealed himself.

The captain, when feeling safe, removed himself from his hiding place and began his trek east again. Deep into the forest, he and another individual spotted each other at the same time and each initially believed the other was an enemy. It was soon realized that the other man was one of Mercer's men. These two continued eastward together, but because of the impenetrability of the forest and lack of food, eventually accepted their fates and gave up. (It must be remembered that Mercer had been wounded at the Kit-Han-Ne battle and undoubtedly had to deal with some loss of blood.) Captain Mercer and the other soldier were discovered and gathered up by Cherokee warriors. These natives transported the two men to Fort Lyttleton. Personally, I believe that many of these missing soldiers and individuals either died in the wilderness or were killed and scalped along the way. I can visualize their scalps drying along a trail-side fire.

Bronze panel set in stone located along the Allegheny River at Kittanning.

Of course, there is no "official" record of native casualties from that September day. Writings of the Pennsylvania Historical and Museum Society of Harrisburg, Pennsylvania, claim that an Indian count was forwarded, with seven men and two women killed. This was, however, only an adult count. Colonel Armstrong estimated that no less than 30 or 40 Indians were killed or mortally wounded. Today we will never know the facts on these figures. As you can see, there is a noticeable difference in the casualty count.

Colonel Armstrong reported that the force had about a dozen scalps and eleven recaptured prisoners during the early hours of their eastbound journey. He also reported that four or five of the scalps were lost along the road. Out of the eleven captives only seven actually were returned home. I do not know if the additional four prisoners that went with Captain Mercer's men ever made the journey back or were recaptured by the natives.

Other people seized from earlier native incursions attempted to flee to safety with Armstrong's army. At least two were retaken by the Delaware while scouring the local forest area. Unfortunately, their fate was not the making of a good family story.

Other prisoners that had been removed from the Indian town at the onslaught of the Kit-Han-Ne battle were returned, only to witness terrible tortures carried out by the natives. Two of the ill-fated victims were a woman (a woman was reported to be with Mercer's men) and an Englishman. Both died horrendous deaths. These acts of torture were done in part as an example to anyone contemplating a future escape. These deeds possibly may have been committed to vent off anger from the attack and the destruction from the battle.

From the Pennsylvania Province standpoint, the attack on the Indian town was a very costly venture. There would not be any additional offensive attacks planned in the future. But the results from the battle did boost a sagging morale among those in the East. However, this boost was short lived— the Indian raids would continue. The colonial people learned, though, that they could effec-

ATTACK ON KIT-HAN-NE

tively fight the Indians and perform well. This fact alone boosted their confidence!

The Delaware and Shawnee of Kit-Han-Ne, though, suffered a loss of confidence in their town area. Some of the natives rebuilt and continued living at the site, at least for a while. How long any natives lived at Kittanning after the battle is unknown. At some time a migration further west became reality for all and the Indian village was abandoned. Many from Kit-Han-Ne moved to other native towns along the Beaver River. Some of these towns were known as Logstown (Ambridge, Beaver County, Pennsylvania), Sauconk (Beaver, Beaver County, Pennsylvania), Kuskuskies (area around New Castle, Pennsylvania) and Shenango (near Sharon, Mercer County, Pennsylvania). Kit-Han-Ne remained an important trail junction for years after the September attack, but it is not believed to have been a meeting place for hostile gatherings during the remainder of the French and Indian War. There is evidence that the town was used during Pontiac's War through the Revolutionary War period as a place to gather for attacks.

In October of 1756 the City of Philadelphia granted 150 pounds to John Armstrong and his officers, to be paid out in pieces of plate, swords and the other things suitable for presents. Some of this fund was to go toward the widows and children of those who died during the Kittanning expedition. The city also cast a medallion representing the battle and honoring those men of the battle. Only a few of the medallions are known to exist today.

The close of the French and Indian War in western Pennsylvania finally came in 1758 after the French troops deserted Fort Duquesne upon learning of the approach of General John Forbes. General Forbes renamed it Fort Pitt (the site of present-day Pittsburgh) in honor of William Pitt, Prime Minister of Great Britain. The natives, as a group, were not beaten by the English army. Many days of peace negotiations and council were the result of the departure of the French forces. The Treaty of Easton in 1758 was generous to the native leaders and peace was secured.

The primary concern of the native tribes, as it had been since the French first invaded their lands, was the removal of all French, English and colonists to the eastern side of the Allegheny Mountain range. These leaders expected the English to keep their word and withdraw their military to the East too. This didn't happen and soon English settlers began a push over the mountains and those in control did little to curtail their actions. France "officially" surrendered their possessions to the English in 1763. The English stayed. A failure to abide by the promises of the treaty was, by this time, a certainty to the native leaders. The results of the failed Treaty of Easton was predictable...Pontiac's War, lead by the great chief Pontiac. This war began in 1763 and in reality was an extension of the French and Indian War. Bushy Run, in Westmoreland County, is a well- known battle site from this period. Pontiac's War ended in 1764.

There was another aspect of the French and Indian War that is seldom mentioned. England, as a result of this war, had become deeply in debt. The British government, in their wisdom, chose to forward the cost of this war to the people of the colonies. Taxes were added and raised, much to the resentment of the American people. Rights were trampled upon by British authorities, and military officers further antagonized the people. So in reality, the closing of the French and Indian War and Pontiac's War would become known as the forerunner to the Revolutionary War. The time frame would cover the years 1764 to 1775. The Declaration of Independence was signed by the thirteen colonies on July 4, 1776.

The War for Independence was now a unstoppable reality! The area around the famous Indian town of Kit-Han-Ne would continue to be an area of warfare and bloodshed.

*A Delaware warrior, painted for terror,
maneuvering through the forest in preparation for battle.*

CHAPTER 8

KIT-HAN-NE: REVOLUTIONARY WAR ERA

Many people today do not realize the extent to which the various Indian tribes participated during the Revolutionary War— the "War for Independence" from England. Most individuals know only of battles fought between colonial and British forces at places, such as Brandywine, Bunker Hill, Princeton and Charleston. They learned of the hardships at Valley Forge. Yet, there was another war happening, the war with the Indians. The truth is, both the British and colonial authorities actively engaged in seeking alliances with the native populations. The various tribes, once again, were caught between the struggles of two powers. The impending circumstances would force many to choose between the "rebel" cause and the powerful British army. Few individuals today realize this war was fought on another front, too. Yes, the Revolutionary War was fought around the Kittanning area, as well as other western Pennsylvania sites.

In July of 1776, with the colonial war for independence now a reality, it became apparent to colonial authorities that the Iroquois people would be siding with the British. Regiments were quickly formed and ordered to strategic spots along the Pennsylvania frontier to build garrisons for defense. These garrisons and others were erected in hopes of protecting the frontier inhabitants from British forces, Tories (Colonial people loyal to the British) and the Iroquois of the North.

One such regiment under the command of Colonel Aeneas Mackey, Lieutenant Colonel George Wilson and Major Richard Butler rendezvoused late in the autumn and built a stockade just below present-day Kittanning. However, these men were ordered to re-

ATTACK ON KIT-HAN-NE

move themselves and join General George Washington's army in January 1777.

To help understand how serious the times were, I must mention that British officer Colonel Henry Hamilton of Fort Detroit (Michigan) was actively inciting the Indians to carry out raids against the colonists. He did this by rewarding them for each scalp presented to him. These Indians, now supplied with another incentive, were heading towards the frontier settlements of western and central Pennsylvania.

CAPTURE OF ANDREW MCFARLANE

Near the site of the Kittanning garrison, Andrew McFarlane conducted a trading post. A company of rangers was organized to protect the supplies left behind by the departing regiment. Apparently few of these rangers actually took continual post at the Kittanning garrison.

On February 14, 1777, two British soldiers, two Chippewas and two Iroquois arrived at the Kittanning area from Fort Niagara. They descended the Allegheny River, hid their canoes and located themselves on the west side of the river opposite McFarlane's trading post. They shouted across the river, in need of a canoe. McFarlane, thinking that these men were in need of trading or, possibly, were carriers of good news, crossed the river and was immediately seized and taken prisoner. He eventually found himself at Quebec. Mrs. McFarlane and the family fled twenty miles to Carnahan's Blockhouse at present-day Bell Township in Westmoreland County.

In 1780 Andrew McFarlane was released after negotiations through his brother and later rejoined his wife to live along Chartiers Creek, Allegheny County for many years. Here he worked a trading post.

KITTANNING, PENNSYLVANIA
INCIDENT AT BLANKET HILL

In March 1777 Fergus Moorhead (sometimes spelled Moorehead) of present-day Indiana County came to the Kittanning garrison to visit his brother Captain Samuel Moorhead, one of the rangers. On March 16th, he and a soldier named Simpson were returning home following the Kittanning Indian Trail. (This is the same trail used by Colonel John Armstrong while en route to attack Kittanning in 1756.) These two men were attacked by Indians near the Blanket Hill area. Fergus Moorhead was captured and Simpson was killed and scalped. Moorhead then was taken to Quebec. Upon his release eleven months later, he said he was treated far worse by British personnel than by the Indians. Samuel Moorhead found the remains of the dead soldier, Simpson, on March 18, 1777.

Fergus Moorhead is memorialized with a mention on the same monument as the "Blanket Hill" skirmish participants. The stone and bronze marker is located on State Route 422 at Blanket Hill, Pennsylvania (see Chapter 6).

The Indian raids became more prevalent along the Pennsylvania frontier during the Revolutionary War period.

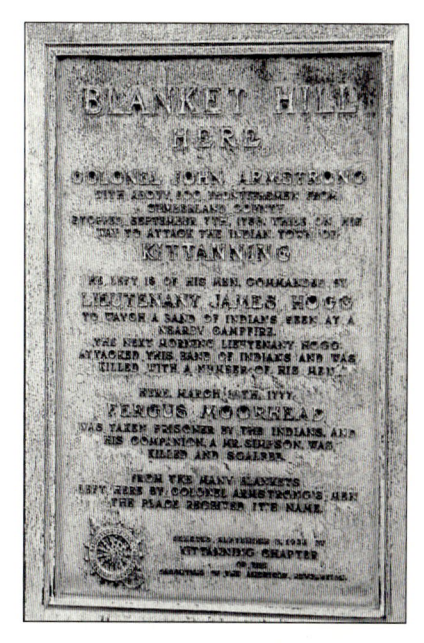

A detail of the bronze marker at Blanket Hill, shown in Chapter 6. The bronze, over the years, has tarnished substantially. In addition to the wording concerning the Blanket Hill battle, the marker mentions the following about the Fergus Moorhead incident: HERE, MARCH 16th, 1777 FERGUS MOORHEAD WAS TAKEN PRISONER BY THE INDIANS AND HIS COMPANION; A MR. SIMPSON WAS KILLED AND SCALPED.

47

ATTACK ON KIT-HAN-NE

Many individuals and families suffered their wrath. In November 1777, some murders were occurring in southwestern Pennsylvania. A party of rangers followed a marauding band of natives. This force overtook the Indians on the east side of the Allegheny River near Kittanning and killed five of the Indians. The rangers returned to the settlers with the scalps of the deceased natives and all stolen horses.

NATIVE AND TORY ACTIVITIES

In an attempt to aid the British war effort, Tories were offering the people of the Pennsylvania mountain areas 500 acres of land and their share of the pillage for anyone deserting the American cause. The catch was that interested individuals had to join a force of British and Indians that was to come down the Allegheny River to Kittanning in the spring of 1778. This force was to organize and proceed south to attack Fort Pitt.

In 1778 a force of Indians gathered at Kittanning and occupied the garrison that was deserted in 1777. Meanwhile, a group of Tories, while en route to Kittanning to converge with these Indians and the promised British and Indian force coming down the Allegheny River, happened on a band of about 100 Iroquois. The Tory leader John Weston ran towards them. These natives, not knowing of the planned conspiracy, killed and scalped Weston before vanishing into the forest. The plans quickly eroded upon the death of Weston. He was buried and the group decided not to proceed any further towards Kittanning.

A group of rangers, upon hearing of the conspiracy to attack Fort Pitt, scoured the woods almost to Kittanning, losing five of their party to murdering natives. The conspiracy continued to rapidly fall apart with some being jailed and others perishing in the wilderness. Some of the conspirators were charged with treason and others escaped to southern British forts.

ATTACK ON THE HENRY FAMILY

In June 1779 a band of natives descended the Allegheny River and attacked the homestead of Frederick Henry (Heinrich), killing Mrs. Henry prior to carrying off three children. One infant who continually cried was killed. Two different accounts of the rescue of the children are on record. The following is from General Daniel Brodhead's report on the recapture of the children:

Captain Samuel Brady and his force of 20 men dressed and painted as Indians and ascended the watershed in search of this group and, hopefully, to recapture the children. Another group of men attempted, but failed, to follow the trail. Brady's force discovered the hidden canoes approximately 15 miles north of Kittanning. The warriors were soon discovered, too. They were preparing their meal on the northern side of Red Bank Creek where this water flows into the Allegheny River (on the Armstrong County and Clarion County border).

Brady's men descended the northern side of the creek close to the encampment and waited under cover of the tall grasses. Brady and his Delaware friend Nanowland crept closer to the camp after dark to gather intelligence regarding the location of the children and the number of natives present.

At daybreak the following morning, Brady and his men attacked the group of natives, killing the chief of the seven warriors and wounding two that fled into the forest with the rest. (One of these wounded Indians was later found dead.) The man killed by Brady was none other than Chief Bald Eagle. Samuel Brady was elated, for he believed that this same native was the one responsible for the killing of James Brady the preceding summer. He had vowed to avenge his brother's death. (East Brady, Pennsylvania, in Clarion County, is located north of this skirmish site and was named after Samuel Brady.) Chief Bald Eagle was a member of the Wolf Clan of the Delaware tribe. Bald Eagle Mountain and Bald Eagle Valley of Clinton and Clearfield Counties are named after the chief. His fol-

ATTACK ON KIT-HAN-NE

lowers raged bloody warfare on the settlements along the west branch of the Susquehanna River.

FORT ARMSTRONG

In the summer of 1779 Colonel Daniel Brodhead begged General Washington for permission to lead an expedition into the northern Seneca country. The purpose of this plan was to strike the Delaware of the Munsee Clan and the Senecas under Guyasuta in their homeland. Brodhead placed a garrison below present-day Kittanning and named it Fort Armstrong in honor of John Armstrong, then General Armstrong. This fort was erected in June 1779.

General Brodhead proceeded north to the mouth of the Mahoning Creek before following an Indian trail farther north, eventually reaching the present-day Kinzua Dam area. This was where the Seneca, under the leadership of Chief Cornplanter, would later reside. The troops returned to Fort Pitt in the early fall of the same year after burning and destroying native homes and acres of corn. Fort Armstrong was abandoned later that same year.

ATTACK ON HANNASTOWN

In July of 1782 Seneca Chief Guyasuta, with approximately 100 warriors and 60 Canadian rangers, navigated the Allegheny River to a point just north of Kittanning. From this point, they traveled on foot towards Hannastown (approximately three miles north of present-day Greensburg, Pennsylvania, in Westmoreland County). Guyasuta and his force, including some British soldiers, attacked, burned the town and killed its occupants. This onslaught proved to be the most devastating Indian attack of the Revolutionary War period.

This was one of innumerable native raids into parts of Pennsylvania during the Revolutionary War period. The area of Kittanning had very few white inhabitants until after this war. The Revolutionary War officially ended in April of 1783.

The Delaware stands by the mighty oak. He is listening and waiting, for he can sense that something is there.

CHAPTER 9

LAST OF NATIVE INCURSIONS

After the close of the Revolutionary War in 1783 the thirteen colonies would become one. That one was and is the United States of America! One might hope at that time that peace would finally become a reality, but that hope would be in vain.

Again, whites and natives came together to sign an agreement, the Treaty of Fort Stanwix (Rome, New York). This time land was ceded with the blessing of Chief Cornplanter of the Seneca. The Seneca were bitter enemies of the United States during the Revolutionary War, but the tribe became a firm friend of the young republic after the war. Kittanning was mentioned a number of times in this deed, for the old Indian town was used as a boundary marker.

Later, in 1787, General Arthur St. Clair was appointed governor of the Northwest Territory. This area included what would become the states of Ohio, Michigan, Wisconsin, Illinois and Indiana. In 1789 St. Clair met with native representatives from a few various tribes at Fort Harmar (mouth of Muskingum River in Ohio). A treaty was signed, with more land being ceded over to the new country. However, a great majority of natives refused to acknowledge the validity of the new treaty.

British agents were busy behind the scenes actively instigating the Indians to revolt. These agents had different ideas for the foundling nation. As you can imagine, the friction resulting from this last treaty worked well with the British activities. The result was again predictable; the natives were again on the war-path. The area of western Pennsylvania would see much animosity as part of these raids. Settlers around the Kittanning area would be victims of their

ATTACK ON KIT-HAN-NE

wrath once more. The new federal government sent troops to the above mentioned areas and Ohio in an attempt to curtail this uprising.

An earlier incident in 1787 or 1788 saw a woman and her brother hoeing corn on the Westmoreland County side of the Kiskiminetas River near present-day Saltsburg, Pennsylvania. The two discovered a number of Indians preparing to ambush; they ran for their lives to a blockhouse nearby and, fortunately, reached safety. The Indians stole most of the horses that night.

The following day, after they felt assured that the natives have left the area, the settlers began to follow their trail. They overtook the natives between Pine Run and present-day Logansport along the Allegheny River (approximately five miles south of Kittanning). The Indians escaped and all but one horse were recaptured.

The natives fled across the river towards the mouth of Nicholson's Run (about one mile south of present-day Cadogan, Pennsylvania, on the west side of the Allegheny River). The warriors followed the Indian trail back toward their towns along the Beaver River.

ATTACK ON THE KIRKPATRICK HOME

In late April 1791, the fortified home of James Kirkpatrick, located in the area of present-day Plum Creek Township, was attacked by three natives. The inhabitants of the house heard a knock on the door. Upon opening the door, Mr. Kirkpatrick was alarmed to see the three painted warriors rush to get in the house. The man slammed the door shut before the intruders could enter. Unfortunately, musket balls were shot into the door, striking a friend of the Kirkpatrick family, George Miller. He was hit in the wrist. Another shot struck a baby in the cradle. This infant later died of the wounds.

Mr. Kirkpatrick quickly climbed into the loft and fired on the Indians, killing one of them. His wife remained by the fire, briskly making lead musket balls while the men defended the house. (One report states that there were two men killed in the house in addition to the baby in the cradle.)

A tradition of the Kirkpatrick family descendants claimed that Mr. Kirkpatrick decapitated the dead native and placed his head on a pole as a deterrent to other Indians considering an attack on his home. Another interesting bit of information concerning the Kirkpatrick incident is that the man skinned the warrior, tanned the hide and made razor straps from the skin. I don't know if any of these "trophies" have survived the years.

FORT RUN TRICKERY

In or around 1791, George Cook resided in what is now Manor Township, Armstrong County. He occupied a fort or blockhouse near the stream called Fort Run (possibly the remnants of the old Fort Armstrong of 1779). He told of an incident where some warriors captured a duck and tethered it with a small cord. They placed the duck into the waters where the Allegheny River and Fort Run intersect. Three white men noticed the duck, which apparently looked like an easy catch. The three leaned their muskets against a tree and proceeded to take this duck. Three shots were heard and the three men were found in the waters of Fort Run…waters that ran red from their blood. The stream was called Bloody Run because of the deaths and circumstances of their demise.

Several men ventured from the safety of their buildings at the report of the muskets. They discovered what had happened and began following the trail of the Indians. The men followed the warriors north along the east side of the Allegheny River through the old Indian town of Kit-Han-Ne. The men discovered a fire on the side of the hill along what is now Pine Creek. They waited until after dark, crossed the creek and closed in towards the fire. At daybreak the men crept to within gun range. The reports claimed one of the natives was mending his moccasins while the other two were busy cooking meat.

ATTACK ON KIT-HAN-NE

At the initial shooting, two of the Indians were killed and the third captured. The men made the captured native an offer to run. He was told he would be given a head start, and if he should outrun them, he would be free. The Indian accepted the offer, but was overtaken and shot.

SLOAN CHILDREN CAPTURED

Child members of the Sloan family were captured near the Kirkpatrick home. This capture occurred within a few weeks of the Kirkpatrick attack. Those taken by the natives were working in a corn field. These children lived with the natives for several years before being delivered to Fort Washington at present-day Cincinnati, Ohio. The children were later returned to their parents in the area of South Bend Township in Armstrong County.

MASSA HARBISON

How would you like to spend everyday of your life watching over your shoulder? Living in the era of the Indian wars would be just like that! Massa (Massy) Harbison was a young woman during that era. Her trials and tribulations are often mentioned during local history discussions. Her ordeal is one of great courage and wit.

Mrs. Harbison was within gunshot range of a blockhouse called Reed's Station (two miles below the mouth of the Kiskiminetas River). On May 22, 1792, Massa was about to endure the most difficult experience of her life when a band of warriors invaded her home. The door was purposely left open by two men often referred to as spies, allowing a band of natives to enter the cabin and drag Massa and her family out of their beds. She ran outside, screaming, towards the blockhouse with one native stopping her and another preparing to dispatch her with his tomahawk. A third interrupted her almost-certain demise by claiming her to become his squaw.

KITTANNING, PENNSYLVANIA

Mrs. Harbison kept her wits when she told the warriors that about 40 men were at the blockhouse, each armed with two muskets. But the band of Indians, while deciding to leave the house, abducted her family. One small child, crying and fighting to remain, was killed and scalped on the spot.

Mrs. Harbison and her remaining two children were taken to the top of the hill east of present-day Freeport, Pennsylvania (Armstrong County) by the band of 32 men. Two of these "natives" were white men painted as warriors. Some of the others she identified as Delaware and Seneca natives. Several had been to her home previously to hire Mr. Harbison for musket repairs. This, of course, was during more peaceful times.

The band tied down their plunder, with all but two leaving to raid elsewhere. The two guards proceeded to a point opposite Todd's Island on the Allegheny River. While descending the hill towards the river a horse faltered, throwing another child from its back, injuring him. After the group reached the island this injured child was tomahawked and scalped too. Natives, when returning from a raiding party, were never patient with the stubborn, the injured or those having difficulty traveling.

The two natives and the remaining two captives completed the crossing and continued on to the Connoquenessing River (two miles north of present-day Butler, Pennsylvania). Along its banks they all made camp.

On May 25th, with one of the guarding Indians away and the other fast asleep, Massa managed to make her escape. The courage to make such a decision and act on it is amazing— the result of her recapture would probably not be pleasant. She carried her baby for two days, heading back towards the Allegheny River. The Indians followed her trail and at one time they were close enough for Mrs. Harbison to hear them. She stuffed cloth into her baby's mouth to keep the little one quiet. This had to be extreme terror!

Mrs. Harbison arrived at the west side of the Allegheny River on May 27th opposite Six Mile Island (just above Sharpsburg and opposite Highland Park near Pittsburgh, Pennsylvania). She was rescued by three white men, who cautiously observed her prior to their approach for any sign that would reveal she was an Indian decoy.

Massa was taken to a home where 150 thorns, by actual count, were removed from her feet and legs. She was soon reunited with her husband in Pittsburgh. Scouts were sent to Todd's Island to locate and bury the son who was killed there.

Massa Harbison died at 67 years of age. Her remains are buried at the Freeport Cemetery.

THE ANDREW SHARP TRAGEDY

Captain Andrew Sharp, an officer of the Revolutionary War under General George Washington, purchased land and lived as a farmer for ten years. He and his wife and family had their home along Crooked Creek in, what is now, Plumcreek Township, Armstrong County. He became concerned when his children needed schooling, but the area was lacking schools or teachers. Because of this reason, Mr. Sharp decided to trade the farm for land in Kentucky near a school.

In the spring of 1794, Captain Sharp, his wife and family of six, along with a number of other families totaling 20 individuals, embarked in their journey down the Kiskiminetas River on a flatboat loaded with supplies. Their plans for the trip were to enter the Allegheny River at present-day Schenley, Pennsylvania, before continuing on through Pittsburgh and descending the Ohio River to Kentucky.

The spring of 1794 produced less water than normal and the low water made the trip more difficult. At a point approximately two miles below present-day Apollo, Pennsylvania, the flatboat traveled over some falls where a canoe became untied. Mr. Sharp tied the flatboat down and began to head back upstream to gather the canoe.

Approximately 1½ hours before sunset, Sharp returned to discover the children busily gathering berries and playing along the

KITTANNING, PENNSYLVANIA

shore and the women preparing the evening meal. A man happened by, announcing to the party of twenty that Indians had been reported nearby. The group discussed their options and decided to travel to the home of a David Hall while gathering up their wares.

Suddenly reports of musket fire echoed through the hollow as a group of natives began firing upon the boat. Captain Sharp was grazed along the forehead, severing his right eyebrow. A Mr. Taylor took off on horseback leaving his family behind.

Captain Sharp was cutting the ropes to free the boat when he received a musket ball in his left side. A second ball entered his right side as he reached for a musket and fired it, killing one of the warriors. The boat, back into navigable waters and free from its bindings, began to swirl in a whirlpool for quite sometime. With each spin around and when there was an opportunity to take aim, the natives fired on the occupants of the boat. Finally, the flatboat freed itself from the whirlpool and began to descend the Kiskiminetas River. The natives followed along the shore for about twelve miles. They shouted to those onboard at various times, ordering them to disembark or they would continue firing on them, killing them all. A Mrs. Conner and her eldest son wished to land the boat and face their attackers in hopes of mercy. Her son appealed to the Indians to come to the boat, for all the men were shot. Sharp rebuked the woman and her son, threatening to shoot either of them if they persisted in their cowardice. At that time this eldest son was shot and fell dead. A Mr. McCoy was also killed. Mr. Conner was severely wounded. For whatever reasons, the natives eventually gave up their sport.

The brave Captain Sharp, due to the loss of blood, became exhausted, forcing his wife to take over control of the boat. Nine miles north of Pittsburgh on the following day, some men were spotted and signaled for assistance. One man left for Pittsburgh to alert a doctor of the arrival of the injured group.

Captain Andrew Sharp suffered severely from his wounds and eventually succumbed to them on July 8, 1794. He was buried with the honors of war. Mrs. Sharp returned to her home along Crooked Creek and remained there for years with her family.

BOY CAPTURED IN ECHO, PENNSYLVANIA

I discovered in the book *Indian Wars of Pennsylvania* a brief reading about a local tradition of the capture of a young boy near present-day Echo (Wayne Township, Armstrong County). Circa 1794 Indians from an unknown tribe caused a disturbance among the pigs near a farmer's barn. Upon hearing the commotion, the father went to investigate. Not finding any problems, he returned to find his son missing. A search failed to find the whereabouts of his son. An Indian, no doubt, captured this boy to replace a deceased member of his personal family. This was a common practice for Native Americans in the loss of someone dear to them.

Many years later, the boy, now a man, returned to his boyhood home. He couldn't speak English very well and couldn't properly pronounce any names from his family. His family had moved on or had passed away. The man, having married an Indian maiden, traveled back to his native family never to return to his home area again.

INDIANS OVERTAKEN NEAR BARNARDS

A family was taken into captivity about the same time of the Echo incident. This capture occurred in what is now Indiana County, Pennsylvania. These natives were pursued and overtaken near present-day Barnards, Pennsylvania (Cowanshannock Township, Armstrong County). Three natives were killed in the skirmish and all captives were returned.

KITTANNING, PENNSYLVANIA

WAR ENDS WITH SIGNING OF TREATY OF GREENVILLE

Native raids occurred at many areas of Pennsylvania during this period of our history. Finally in 1795, General "Mad" Anthony Wayne defeated the natives at the Battle of Fallen Timbers in Ohio. With the signing of the Treaty of Greenville of the same year, the conquered tribes and the American people were at last at peace. The treaty ceded 25,000 square miles of former native lands. The fighting between the whites and the Indians had now ceased in the area of Kittanning and the western parts of Pennsylvania. Unfortunately, the future would not see the fighting stopped elsewhere. The battles continued moving west as tribe after tribe would be driven out and more land would be ceded by treaty or conquest. Time continues on!

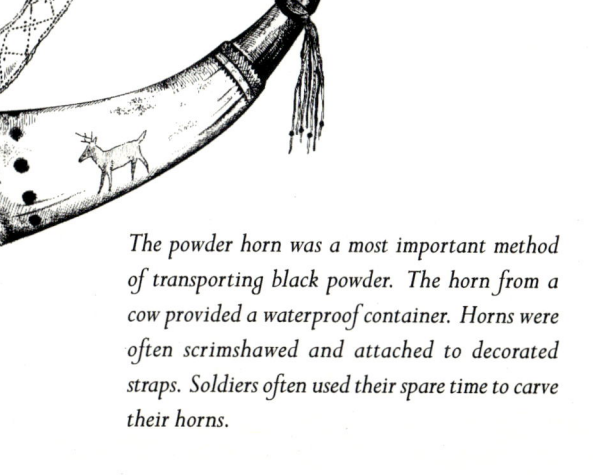

The powder horn was a most important method of transporting black powder. The horn from a cow provided a waterproof container. Horns were often scrimshawed and attached to decorated straps. Soldiers often used their spare time to carve their horns.

61

ATTACK ON KIT-HAN-NE

The wild turkey was a source of food and feather adornments for the Eastern tribes. Warriors often used the vocal sounds of the turkey as a means to communicate among themselves in war.

CHAPTER 10

AUTHOR'S THOUGHTS

I cannot begin to count the hours I have spent searching for information concerning the Delaware town of Kit-Han-Ne and those people associated with it during the 18th century. In many aspects, this venture has been a life-long quest. I hungrily read and absorb any bit of knowledge I can obtain. I talk to others with similar interests whenever an opportunity presents itself, all of this in an attempt to gain more insight on the subject. The time spent has been worthwhile, and I have enjoyed the search despite the frequent frustration of encountering "dead ends" because of the inadequate record keeping of the time. These emotions and thoughts have no recourse but to surface and play on one's mind.

Obviously, I feel a sense of great sadness for those many Delaware and Shawnee people. I feel and understand their pain as I, too, watch the lands that I love and respect lose to development and the continually increasing "sprawl." I can only imagine how one must feel when forced into a war mode due to injustices upon injustices! On the other hand, I feel much sympathy for all those early colonists who settled into Indian lands believing that this was agreeable to all and safe to commit to. I believe these individuals were naive in the entire scenario of that which was happening about them. I have difficulty imagining the troubles and death witnessed by so many. These settlers, like the natives, were caught up amidst the fight of the "big powers."

The times were difficult indeed!

Inevitably, my feelings drift back to the current times. As I stated in my introduction, our society and that of 250 years ago are

ATTACK ON KIT-HAN-NE

very similar. I find it easy to see the same scenario being played out again and again. This consists of those with the power and funds, taking what they want, in contrast to those that have little, with no recourse but to sit back and allow it to happen. The greed factor of yesterday still exists!

As I have mentioned, I cringe when I witness "progress" continuing to engulf the woodlands and farms at an ever increasing rate. I have seen many hills lost, due to a society desperate for energy. I have witnessed acres upon acres of valuable farmland absorbed into the development of housing plans and malls. I see a society that demands forests without big trees. The logging trucks of today, often, have smaller and smaller diameter trees loaded on their beds. Have you noticed? Woodland areas are becoming increasingly fragmented and smaller. Yet, our society and government (usually for political gains) continue to further divide lands with more road building. One of the disadvantages of having a number of years of life behind you is witnessing these many drastic changes over a relatively short amount of time and knowing the problems associated with those changes.

The society of today has become indifferent to much of its roots. When I was a boy, practically every male and some females

The white-tailed deer was a very important food source for both the early colonists and Indians. Clothing and moccasins were made from the tanned hides of deer. Deer fur, antlers, bones and hooves were used for decorating.

actively hunted and fished. Many trapped. Today, these individuals are often looked upon as a cruel and despicable people. Then, school boys always carried pocket knives. Today, finger nail clippers may lead to a suspension from school! There are those that believe the United States Constitution implies that praying in a government building is a violation of immense magnitude. These individuals say to do so is a crime because of the "separation of church and state." Again, read the documents for yourself, learn the history as to what the original intent was. The intent was to keep a government from abusing its power by claiming an official denomination. The Founding Fathers knew how governments across the sea had committed such an abuse. People were tortured and/or killed for failing to adhere to the policies of a one-denominational church. Our founders did not wish a repeat of such laws in their new country. The rationalization on this subject is plain and simple without the current distortion! I cannot imagine what people of twenty years into the future may witness if the current trend of "political correctness" grows in acceptance. Mankind, with the same scenes being played out generation after generation, has learned little.

The anti-gun movement is continually attempting to erode away the Second Amendment rights that are permanently guaranteed by our United States Constitution. Do you need proof of what our Founding Fathers meant by the Second Amendment? Read some of these quotes:

"Firearms stand next in importance to the Constitution itself. They are the American people's liberty teeth and keystone under independence. To ensure peace, security, and happiness, the rifle and pistol are equally indispensable. The very atmosphere of firearms everywhere restrains evil interference. They deserve a place of honor with all that's good."

- George Washington

"To preserve liberty it is essential that the whole body of the people always possess arms and be taught alike, especially when young, how to use them..."

- Richard Henry Lee

"The right of the people to keep and bear...arms shall not be infringed. A well regulated militia, composed of the people, trained to arms is the best

and most natural defense of a free country..."

- James Madison

"The constitution shall never be construed to authorize Congress...to prevent the people of the United States who are peaceable citizens from keeping their own arms."

- Samuel Adams

"And what country can preserve its liberties, if its rulers are not warned time to time, that this people preserve the spirit of resistance? Let them take arms...The Tree of Liberty must be refreshed from time to time, with the blood of patriots and tyrants."

- Thomas Jefferson

"No free man shall ever be debarred the use of arms. The strongest reason for the people to retain the right to keep and bear arms is, as a last resort, to protect themselves against tyranny in government."

- Thomas Jefferson

These are but a few quotes from the Founding Fathers of our country...the United States of America. I believe their words leave no doubt as to their original intent! It must be remembered that these and many other individuals debated and finalized the constitution and the Bill of Rights. They were men of great wisdom and understanding, for they witnessed tyranny first-hand! Wave the flag proudly!

The era of the French and Indian War through the Revolutionary War period seems like a distant dream to most Americans today. Many may actually doubt that such a magnitude of death and destruction could have been possible. It is commonly believed this type of killing and treachery could only occur in foreign countries or out in the plains of the old West. Could there have actually been "Indians" here in the eastern forests of Pennsylvania? Of course the answer is a resounding yes.

Native Americans are often referred to as being the first conservationists. I believe that in many aspects this attribution indeed was true. Obviously, when one's survival depends on wildlife for food and the land for crops, a bond of respect would be natural and

KITTANNING, PENNSYLVANIA

important to keep. You can readily understand why the natives would go to war for their "lands." They respected and loved the ground and the trees and all the "critters." Many of the colonists of the era felt this same bond. One could call it a supreme reverence for the natural world.

My goal, upon writing this book, was to introduce readers to the era of the 18th century and the people and places associated with the Indian village of Kittanning. I trust that an open mind was in play throughout this reading so that the circumstances and situations of the times begin to form honest opinions and understanding. In our world today, obtaining factual and honest information through the media is rare. Unfortunately, distorted biases are the norm. The same issue concerning honest information today was commonplace in those early years. I would suspect that facts would have been even more difficult to obtain given the means of recording and receiving information and the length of time it took to be delivered. For a society to act properly and correctly and make good decisions to benefit the people and the country, factual and honest information is a must. Our job is to not believe what we hear as gospel without much thought and analyzing.

It is my hope that the pages within these chapters have enlightened you, the reader. I hope a desire to continue a study into the people, places and events of 18th century Kittanning exists. As stated earlier, there are many books available to help you continue on the journey of our history. Many book options are listed in the bibliography. And today, in our modern society, internet, video and DVD technology provide quick access to an abundance of information, further enabling you to discover the past.

I urge you to continue the quest.

Thank you ....Larry Smail

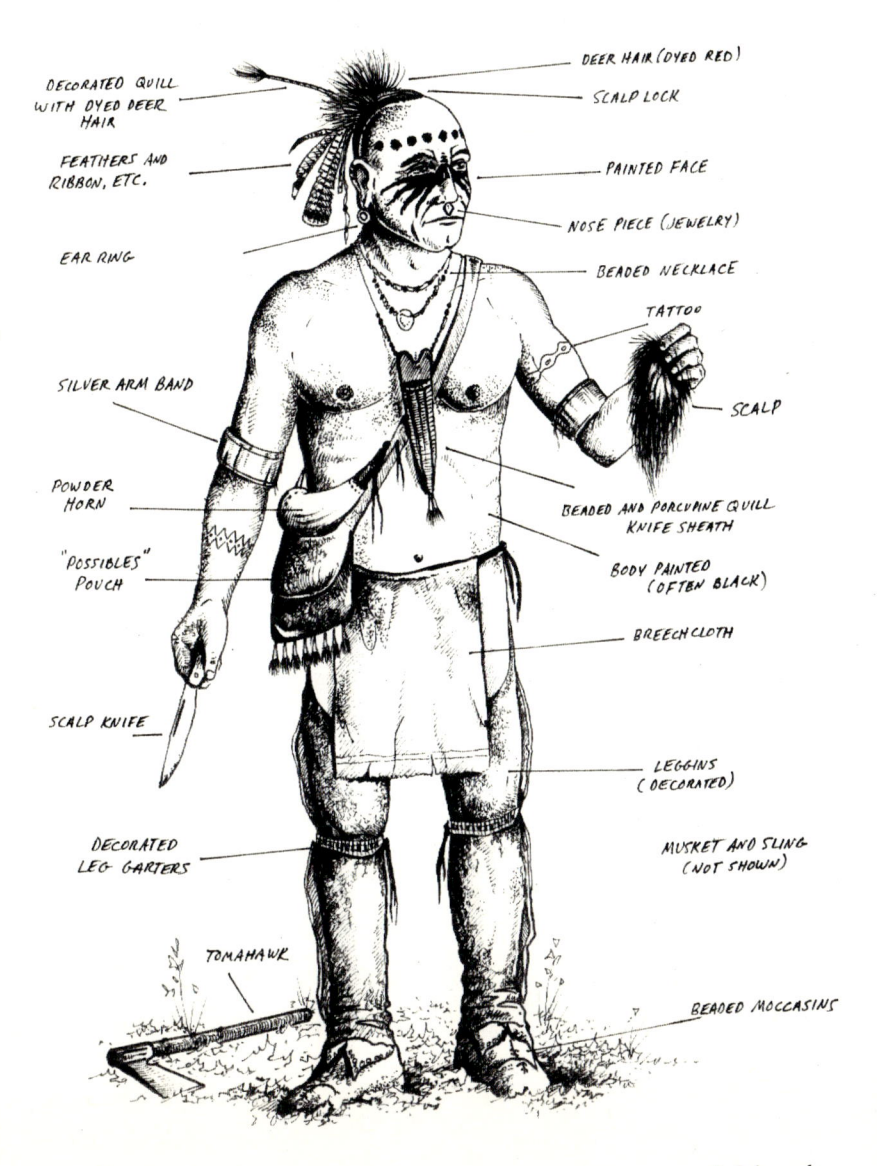

Delaware warrior in all his splendor. Individual personalities were revealed through paint colors and decorating styles.

1756- Fort Granville burns under Captain Jacobs; the attack on Kit-Han-Ne; Blanket Hill skirmish; Pennsylvania declares war on natives of Kit-Han-Ne and elsewhere.

1758- French abandon Fort Duquesne to General Forbes; Treaty of Easton signed; Kit-Han-Ne natives stop raids.

1763- Treaty of Easton not abided by; Pontiac's War begins.

1764- Pontiac's War ends.

1775- Revolutionary War begins.

1776- Declaration of Independence is signed; Iroquois nations ally with the British.

1787-1782- Native incursions into frontier settlements

1783- Revolutionary War "officially" ends.

1787-1795- Native incursions into western Pennsylvania

1795- Battle of Fallen Timbers; Treaty of Greenville ends native incursions.

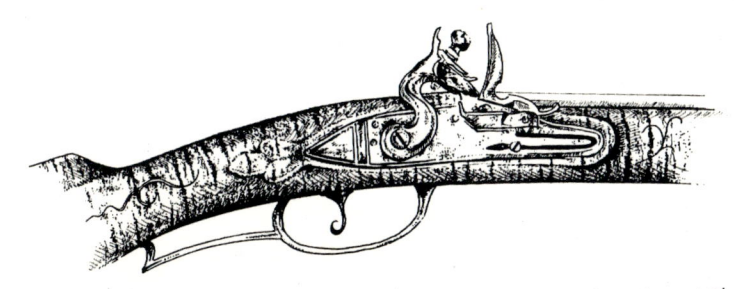

A drawing of the flintlock mechanism found in all firearms of the later 18th century. Black (priming) powder was added to the pan, the hammer was cocked and the trigger squeezed. The flint, which is anchored in the hammer, would strike the frizzen, pushing it ahead. The resulting hot spark fell into the pan powder, thus igniting the primary powder charge within the breech of the barrel.

CHRONOLOGICAL TABLE

1682- William Penn sets sail from England for his new Pennsylvania Province.

1718- William Penn dies.

1723-1730- Time frame of early Delaware migration and establishment of Kit-Han-Ne

1731- White traders in Kit-Han-Ne and western Pennsylvania; Captain Hill is chief at Kit-Han-Ne.

1737- Signing of the infamous Walking Purchase Treaty

1742- Western migration for the Wolf Clan of the Delaware natives to Kit-Han-Ne

1744- Treaty of Lancaster

1748- Ohio Company land speculators are formed.

1749- French Expedition descends the Allegheny River, burying lead plates at various places to claim the lands for the Crown of France.

1753- Virginia governor sends George Washington to petition the French to leave the lands.

1754- Washington and Seneca Chief Half King defeats French troops but later surrenders to the French at Fort Necessity. French and Indian War begins with these actions.

1755- General Braddock is soundly defeated; Kit-Han-Ne natives ally with French; native incursions begin through the Pennsylvania frontier; Penn's Creek Massacre.

BIBLIOGRAPHY

Donehoo, George P. *Pennsylvania: A History, Volume 2.* Lewis Historical Publishing Company, 1926.

Downes, Randolph C. *Council Fires on the Upper Ohio,* Pittsburgh, Pa.: University of Pittsburgh Press, 1940, 1969 Reprint.

Hunter, William P. *Forts on the Pennsylvania Frontier 1753-1758,* Lewisburg, Pa.: Wennawoods Publishing, 1960, 1999 Reprint.

Loudon, Archibald *Loudon's Indian Narratives,* Lewisburg, Pa.: Wennawoods Publishing, 1808, 1996 Reprint.

McConnell, Michael N. *A Country between the Upper Ohio Valley and Its People, 1724-1774.* University of Nebraska Press, 1992.

Rupp, I.D. *Early History of Western Pennsylvania,* Lewisburg, Pa.: Wennawoods Publishing, 1846, 1995 Reprint.

Sipes, C. Hale. *The Indian Chiefs of Pennsylvania,* Lewisburg, Pa.: Wennawoods Publishing, 1927, 1997 Reprint.

Sipes, C. Hale. *The Indian Wars of Pennsylvania,* Lewisburg, Pa.: Wennawoods Publishing, 1931, 1998 Reprint.

Wallace, Paul A. *Armstrong's Victory At Kittanning,* Harrisburg, Pa.: Pennsylvania Historical & Museum Commission, 1995 Reprint.

Wallace, Paul A. *Indians in Pennsylvania,* Harrisburg, Pa.: Pennsylvania Historical & Museum Commission, 1961.

Wallace, Paul A., editor. *The Travels of John Heckewelder in Frontier America,* Pittsburgh, Pa.: University of Pittsburgh Press, 1958.

Some native warriors also used war clubs in place of a tomahawk. The war club was carved from wood (often maple, for strength) and decorated and painted. Some users anchored metal points to the ball end to further ensure the potency as a lethal weapon.